Peiresc's *History of Provence*

Antiquarianism and the Discovery
of a Medieval Mediterranean

Peiresc's *History of Provence*
Antiquarianism and the Discovery
of a Medieval Mediterranean

❧

Peter N. Miller

American Philosophical Society
Philadelphia • 2011

Transactions of the
American Philosophical Society
Held at Philadelphia
For Promoting Useful Knowledge
Volume 101, Part 3

Library of Congress Cataloging-in-Publication Data

Miller, Peter N., 1964-
  Peiresc's History of Provence : antiquarianism and the discovery of a medieval
Mediterrranean / Peter N. Miller.
    p. cm. — (Transactions of the American Philosophical Society Held at Philadelphia for
Promoting Useful Knowledge, ISSN 0065-9746 ; v. 101, pt. 3)
  Includes bibliographical references and index.
  ISBN 978-1-60618-013-6
  1. Peiresc, Nicolas Claude Fabri de, 1580–1637. Abrégé de l'histoire de Provence et
autres textes inédits. 2. Peiresc, Nicolas Claude Fabri de, 1580–1637—Criticism and
interpretation. 3. Provence (France)—Historiography. 4. Mediterranean Region—History—
476–1517—Historiography. 5. Antiquarians—France—History—17th century. 6.
Historiography—France—History—17th century. 7. Learning and scholarship—France—
History—17th century. I. Title.
  DC611.P964P4536 2011
  944.9—dc23
                          2011046250

For the Samuel Miller who this year is seven (and remembering the Samuel Miller who would have been one hundred)

Contents

❖

Acknowledgments

✤

Preliminary forms of this argument were presented to the BGC/Columbia Medieval-Renaissance Seminar in May 2008; the Early Modern History workshop at Princeton University in April 2010; and at the Whitney Humanities Center, Yale University, in May 2010. I benefited much from the lively exchanges and am grateful to all who attended, and especially to those who invited me. Brigitte Bedos-Rezak, Adam J. Kosto, Jacob Soll, and Orest Ranum read and commented on earlier versions of the written text, for which they have my deepest appreciation. Marc Fumaroli, Tony Grafton, Alain Schnapp, and Jérôme Delatour have been part of a long-running conversation with me about Peiresc, and it is a pleasure to thank them yet again for all that they have given me. If there is one book that has inspired me at many different stages of my thinking ever since I was an undergraduate, and which, I realize now that it is finished, marks this project as well, it is John Pocock's *Ancient Constitution and the Feudal Law*.

I have been helped by many librarians and archivists over the years. I would like to signal the special consideration I have received from the late Isabelle Battez, Christiane Imbert, and Jean-François Delmas, who have been the conservators of the Bibliothèque Inguimbertine at Carpentras during the years I have worked there on Peiresc materials. I am especially grateful to M. Delmas for his commitment to furthering access to Peiresc's archive. Michel de Laburthe at the Bibliothèque Méjanes in Aix and Mireille Pastoureau at the Bibliothèque de l'Institut in Paris also deserve special thanks. At home, the staff of Bard Graduate Center's library has been unfailingly helpful in dealing with requests for books and loans: Heather Topcik, Karyn Hinkle, and Janis Ekdahl in particular. I am grateful to Mary McDonald of the American Philosophical Society, and Pamela Lankas of IGS, for the patience and unfailing courtesy that has made work on the final steps of this project so easy.

This book is dedicated to my son, but it is the life of my whole family these last years—Deborah and Livia, as well as Sam—that has surely found its way into every word, mood, and tense.

List of Illustrations

❖

"Aristoteles et Peireskius credunt..."
—Leibniz, *Protogaea*

"Peiresc, l'homme de la civilisation"
—Michelet, *Journal 1828–48*

I

Introduction: Peiresc and Antiquarianism

⚜

THE PROBLEM OF ANTIQUARIANISM can no longer be dismissed as one of only "antiquarian" interest. It has emerged in the past two decades as lying athwart several key axes of the scholarly interpretation of early modern Europe. Antiquarianism has become important for helping us understand the relationships between philology and history,[1] antiquities and art history,[2] and empiricism and the New Science.[3] The social world of learning in which antiquarian life was a part was the Republic of Letters, and this group, too, has become central to genealogies of modern civil society.[4] Building on the classic work of the Italian historian of the ancient world and its modern study, Arnaldo Momigliano, "antiquarianism" is now seen as mediating between different kinds of historical scholarship. Momigliano, in a seemingly straightforward but actually highly complex way, contrasted the rhetorical mode of the writers of ancient history with structural accounts built on research into specific aspects of daily life in the ancient world.[5]

Following Momigliano, either explicitly or implicitly, those who have studied early modern antiquaries and antiquarianism have explored the relationship between textual, visual, and material evidence. Their sensitive probing has made an enormous contribution to our understanding of historical scholarship and its relationship to the revival of antiquity.[6] In turn, the study of the past no longer appears so distinct from the study of nature or of living peoples elsewhere in the world. Indeed, if we look closely, and know what it is we are looking for, we find the practice and perspective of antiquarianism present wherever people pay attention to the past.[7] A paradox inherent in the study of antiquarianism "in context" is, then, that the more places we find it, the less specific its meaning, yet if we narrowly define antiquarianism in terms of practices such as reading inscriptions, we risk missing its broader relevance.

Nicolas Fabri de Peiresc (1580–1637; Figure 1.1) exemplifies the challenge of studying early modern European antiquarianism.[8] He collected an enormous number of different kinds of ancient artifacts and studied them collaboratively. He read ancient texts and annotated them. He compared texts and artifacts to answer questions either elusive or invisible when approached from within only one field or medium. But Peiresc also applied the methodological principles he used for studying the classical past—Greece and Rome—to studying the Biblical and postclassical Mediterranean. And, he drew on this same tool kit when he studied natural history and distant peoples. From this perspective he exemplifies the "greater" antiquarianism—did Momigliano have this in mind when he pronounced Peiresc "that archetype of all antiquaries"?—and helps us see the connections between a narrower study of the ancient world and the large-scale epistemological revolution of the period 1550–1650.[9]

The most obviously extraordinary aspect of Peiresc's intellectual practice was his range: from astronomy to zoology and from ancient Greece to modern

FIGURE 1.1   Nicolas Fabri de Peiresc. Engraving by Lucas Vorsterman, after Jan Van Dyck. Private Collection.

Yemen. Less obvious but perhaps more significant was his marvelous ability to wring information out of a text or object by asking the right question, or framing the right comparison. He often described this as "conjecture," and asked his interlocutors' forgiveness for indulging in it.[10] We might term this facility the "evidentiary imagination" and, rather, admire Peiresc's ability to see meaning where others had previously found only matter. It is in his medieval studies that this skill may appear most clearly because the greater range of surviving materials enabled him to discover more documentary possibilities than were available when investigating the ancient or extra-European worlds. From this perspective, too, we can discern connections between Peiresc and later seventeenth-century titans of medieval studies such as Mabillon and Leibniz, and through them to the modern historical auxiliary sciences (*historische Hilfswissenschaften*) and beyond.[11]

Peiresc wrote constantly. The 60,000-odd pages of surviving manuscript material include reading notes, memoranda, shopping lists, excerpta, and thousands upon thousands of letters. Because he rejected publication in print, and because antiquarianism for so long was not a subject of scholarship, these papers and their structure have remained intact, like some forgotten ancient site awaiting its archaeologist. This long preservation *in situ* — spared the destructive ravages of well-intentioned but underinformed inquirers of an earlier age — makes the Peiresc archive an extraordinary resource for examining antiquarian scholarship as practiced and lived.

If the first generations of modern scholarship focused on Peiresc operated in survey mode — I have in mind the editions of Tamizey de Larroque and the overviews of Raymond Lebègue[12] — by far the most important work of the last few decades has come from those who have focused on Peiresc and the "revival of antiquity" — Agnès Bresson and David Jaffé in particular.[13] Yet it was the history, languages, and literature of the Levant, what we might call "late Renaissance Oriental studies," that captivated Peiresc in his intellectual maturity. The explorations he undertook and encouraged in the decade and a half between his return to Aix from Paris in October 1623 and his death in June 1637 extended late humanist philological tools to the world of the eastern Mediterranean. The connection of the Biblical Near East to the Greco-Roman Mediterranean was one focus; the later cultural transformations effected by Hellenism and Islam was another.[14] That Peiresc was able to make such a dramatic impact on the shape of European learning reflects not only his intellectual vision but signals a real practical understanding of, and ability to exploit, the Mediterranean reach of Provençal merchants and shipping.[15] Among seventeenth-century scholars, Peiresc's intellectual life was probably more part of the "portuary complex" than any other. Peiresc's Orient, in short, was connected to Europe by Peiresc's Mediterranean.

The essay that follows, like most of what I write about Peiresc, is intended to work on three levels, with three goals (and perhaps three audiences). On one level, it is a work of philology: What did he say? What did he do and when? Its ambition is to reconstruct Peiresc's study of the human history of the Mediterranean in the Middle Ages.[16] It was his commitment to studying the medieval history of Provence, a subject dear to him as a local patriot, which in turn connected to this broader story. On a second level, this essay is about context, using the philological recovery to reassess a historical problem. The story of Peiresc and the medieval Mediterranean shows us how he worked when thinking historically. This points us toward the role of archives, material evidence, and the Middle Ages in the world of seventeenth-century antiquaries. This contributes to the ongoing discussion of early modern scholarly practice. On a third level, once we see what Peiresc did, and how he did it, we perceive that a bigger story to which it belongs—the history of antiquarianism— intersects with the history of historical scholarship in ways that have not yet been appreciated. From the unlikely platform of Peiresc's study of the medieval Mediterranean we can discern, in the broadest possible brushstrokes, the outlines of a very different history of history for the period 1500–2000, one organized around research rather than writing. This third layer, to which we will return at the end of this volume, raises questions of orientation and descent that all practicing historians might want to consider.

Notes

[1] Arnaldo Momigliano, "L'eredità della filologia antica e il metodo storico," *Secondo contributo alla storia degli studi classici* (Roma: Edizioni di Storia e Letteratura, 1960), 463–480; Benedetto Bravo, *Philologie, histoire, philosophie de l'histoire. Étude sur J.G. Droysen historien de l'antiquité* (Hildesheim: Georg Olms, 1988 [1968]); Anthony Grafton, *Joseph Scaliger: A Study in the History of Classical Scholarship*, 2 vols. (Oxford: Oxford University Press, 1983–1993); Helmut Zedelmaier, *Bibliotheca universalis und bibliotheca selecta: das Problem der Ordnung des gelehrten Wissens in der frühen Neuzeit* (Cologne: Böhlau, 1992). A powerful recent demonstration of the historical capability of early modern philology is found in Ralph Häfner, *Götter im Exil: Frühneuzeitliches Dichtungsverständnis im Spannungsfeld christlicher Apologetik und philologischer Kritik (ca. 1590–1736)* (Tübingen: Niemeyer, 2003).

[2] Francis Haskell, *History and its Images: Art and the Interpretation of the Past* (New Haven: Yale University Press, 1993); Ingo Herklotz, *Cassiano dal Pozzo und die Archäologie des 17. Jahrhunderts* (Munich: Hirmer, 1999); David Freedberg, *The Eye of the Lynx: Galileo, His Friends, and the Beginnings of Modern Natural History* (Chicago: University of Chicago Press, 2002); *Documentary Culture: Florence and Rome from Grand-Duke Ferdinand I to Pope Alexander VII*, Elizabeth Cropper, Giovanna Perini, and Francesco Solinas, eds. (Bologna: Nuova Alfa Editoriale, 1992); Francesco Solinas, ed. *Cassiano dal Pozzo: Atti del Seminario internazionale di studi* (Rome: De Luca,1989); Francesco Solinas, ed., *I segreti di un collezionista: le straordinarie raccolte di Cassiano dal Pozzo 1588–1657* (Rome: Edizioni De Luca, 2000).

[3] Pamela O. Long, *Openness, Secrecy, Authorship: Technical Arts and the Culture of Knowledge from Antiquity to the Renaissance* (Baltimore: Johns Hopkins University Press, 2001); Paula Findlen, *Possessing Nature: Museums, Collecting, and Scientific Culture in Early Modern Italy* (Berkeley: University of California Press, 1994); Pamela H. Smith, *Body of the Artisan: Art and Experience in the Scientific Revolution* (Chicago: University of Chicago Press, 2004); Harold J. Cook, *Matters of Exchange: Commerce, Medicine, and Science in the Dutch Golden Age* (New Haven: Yale University Press, 2007); Nancy G. Siraisi, *History, Medicine, and the Traditions of Renaissance Learning* (Ann Arbor: University of Michigan Press, 2007); Nancy G. Siraisi and Gianna Pomata, eds., *'Historia': Empiricism and Erudition in Early Modern Europe* (Cambridge, MA: MIT Press, 2005).

[4] Marc Fumaroli, *L'Age de l'éloquence: Rhétorique et "res literaria", de la Renaissance au seuil de l'époque classique* (Geneva: Droz, 1980); Wilhelm Kühlmann, *Gelehrtenrepublik und Fürstenstaat: Entwicklung und Kritik des deutschen Späthumanismus in der Literatur des Barockzeitalters* (Tübingen: Niemeyer, 1982); Marvin B. Becker, *Civility and Society in Western Europe, 1300–1600* (Bloomington: Indiana University Press, 1982); idem, *The Emergence of Civil Society in the Eighteenth Century: A Privileged Moment in the History of England, Scotland, and France* (Bloomington: Indiana University Press, 1994); Anne Goldgar, *Impolite Learning: Conduct and Community in the Republic of Letters, 1680–1750* (New Haven: Yale University Press, 1994).

[5] Arnaldo Momigliano, "Ancient History and the Antiquarian," *Journal of the Warburg and Courtauld Institutes*, 13 (1950), 285–315; *Classical Foundations of Modern Historiography* (Berkeley: University of California Press, 1990), chp. 3: "The Rise of Antiquarian Research." See, for an overview, Ingo Herklotz, "Arnaldo Momigliano's 'Ancient History and the Antiquarian': A Critical Review," *Momigliano and Antiquarianism: Foundations of the Modern Cultural Sciences*, Peter N. Miller, ed. (Toronto: University of Toronto Press, 2007), 127–153; Markus Völkel, "Historischer Pyrrhonismus und Antiquarismus-Konzeption bei Arnaldo Momigliano," *Historischer Pyrrhonismus*, Gisela Schlüter, ed. (= *Das Achtzehnte Jarhrhundert* 31), (Wolfenbüttel: Wallstein, 2007), 179–190.

[6] *Archäologie der Antike. Aus den Beständen der Herzog August Bibliothek, 1500–1700*, Margaret Maly Davis, ed. (Wiesbaden: Harrassowitz, 1994); Alain Schnapp, *La conquête du passé. Aux origines de l'archéologie* (Paris: Editions Carré, 1993); William Stenhouse, *Reading Inscriptions & Writing Ancient History. Historical Scholarship in the Late Renaissance* (London: Institute of Classical Studies, University of London School of Advanced Study, 2005); Anna Schreurs, *Antikenbild und Kunstanschauungen des Pirro Ligorio (1513–1583)* (Bonn: W. König, 2000); Jean-Louis Ferrary, *Onofrio Panvinio et les antiquités romaines* (Rome: Ecole française de Rome, 1996); *Antiquarische Gelehrsamkeit und Bildende Kunst. Die Gegenwart der Antike in der Renaissance*, Katharina Corsepius et al., eds. (Bonn: W. König, 1996).

[7] A direct comparison of European and Chinese antiquarianism is the subject of *Antiquarianism and Intellectual Life in Europe and China, 1500–1800*, François Louis and Peter N. Miller, eds. (Ann Arbor: University of Michigan Press, 2012); a global

survey of antiquarianisms is undertaken in *World Antiquarianism*, Alain Schnapp, ed. (Los Angeles: Getty Publications, 2012).

[8] For biographical surveys, see Pierre Gassendi, *Viri Illustris Nicolai Claudii Fabricii de Peiresc Senatoris Aquisextiensis Vita* (Paris: Sebastiani Cramoisy, 1641); Pierre Humbert, *Un amateur: Peiresc, 1580–1637* (Paris: Desclée de Brouwer, 1933); Henri Leclerq, "Peiresc," *Dictionnaire d'archéologie chrétien et de liturgie*, F. Cabrol, ed., 15 vols. (Paris: Letouzey et Ané, 1939), XIV, 1–39; Raymond Lebègue, *Les correspondants de Peiresc dans les anciens Pays-Bas* (Brussels: Office de publicité, 1943); Marc Fumaroli, *Nicolas-Claude Fabri de Peiresc, prince de la République des lettres* (Brussels: Pro Peyresq, 1993); Peter N. Miller, *Peiresc's Europe: Learning and Virtue in the Seventeenth Century* (New Haven: Yale Unversity Press, 2000). For a full bibliography see http://peiresc.wikis.bgc.bard.edu/peiresc-bibliography.

[9] Momigliano, *Classical Foundations*, 54. Anthony Grafton and Joanna Weinberg describe him as "the brilliant young dean of antiquaries in his own time." (*'I have always loved the Holy Tongue.' Isaac Casaubon, the Jews, and a Forgotten Chapter in Renaissance Scholarship*. Cambridge, MA: Belknap Press, 2011, 16).

[10] A century later, another antiquarian described the "pays des conjectures" as "un pays perdus," reminding us just how unusual was Peiresc's openness to possibility. (Odile Cavalier, "Un Sanctuaire de la mémoire: Le cabinet de cuirosités d'Esprit Calvet (1728–1810)" in *Les Antiquaires du Midi: Savoirs et Mémoirs XVIe–XIXe Siècle*, Véronique Krings and Catherine Valenti, eds. Paris: éditions errance, 2010, 42).

[11] These connections are not visible in today's *Handbücher*, viz. R.C. van Caenegem et al., *Introduction aux sources de l'histoire médiévale* (Turnhut: Brepols, 1997), Pt 3, ch. 1 "Introduction historique." The role of Leibniz, however, is singled out in Henri Berr and Lucien Febvre, "History and Historiography," *Encyclopaedia of the Social Sciences*, Edwin R. A. Seligman, ed. (New York: Macmillan, 1937), 363–364. For Peiresc and Mabillon, see Miller, "Peiresc and the Benedictines of Saint-Maur: Further Thoughts on the 'Ethics of the Historian.'" *Europäische Geschichtskulturen um 1700 zwischen Gelehrsamkeit, Politik und Konfession*, Thomas Wallnig, Ines Peper, Thomas Stockinger, and Patrick Fiska, eds. (Berlin: De Gruyter, 2012). The extended story from Peiresc to Leibniz and on through the development of the *historische Hilfswissenschaft* into the nineteenth century is the subject of my *Cultural History Before Burckhardt: An Essay on the Foundations of Material Culture* (in progress).

[12] Tamizey de Larroque, ed., *Lettres de Peiresc* (Paris: Imprimerie Nationale, 1888–1898), 7 vols.; idem, *Les Correspondants de Peiresc* (Geneva: Stakine Reprints, 1972), 2 vols.; Lebègue, *Les correspondants de Peiresc dans les anciens Pays-Bas*; idem, "État Présent des études Peiresciennes", *Revue Archéologique* 40 (1952), 55–63.

[13] For example, Agnès Bresson, "Peiresc et le commerce des Antiquités à Rome," *Gazette des Beaux-Arts* 135 (1975), 61–72; idem, "Peiresc et le cercle humaniste d'Augsbourg," *Peiresc (1604–2004), Actes du Colloque International, 26–30 Août 2004*, Jean Dhombres and Agnès Bresson, eds. (Turnhout: Brepols, 2006), 173–258; and David Jaffé, "Aspects of Gem Collecting in the Early Seventeenth Century, Nicolas-Claude Peiresc and Lelio Pasqualini," *The Burlington Magazine* 135 (1993), 103–120; "Peiresc and New Attitudes to Authenticity in the Seventeenth Century," *Why Fakes Matter: Essays on Problems of Authenticity*, Mark Jones, ed. (London: British Museum

Press, 1993), 157–173. Antiquity also figures largely as the subject of the bilateral correspondences published in the 1980s and 1990s: Peiresc's with Cassiano dal Pozzo (*Lettres à Cassiano dal Pozzo*, Jean-François Lhote and Danielle Joyal, eds. Clermont-Ferrand: Adosa, 1989); with Saumaise (*Lettres à Claude Saumaise et à son entourage (1620–1637)*, Agnès Bresson, ed. Florence: Leo S. Olschki, 1992; and Aleandro (*Correspondance de Peiresc & Aleandro 1616–1620*, Jean-François Lhote and Danielle Joyal, eds., 2 vols. Clermont-Ferrand: Adosa, 1995). Now, also see Francesco Solinas, ed., *Les correspondances de Nicolas-Claude Fabri de Peiresc (1580–1637) et Monseigneur Lelio Pasqualini (1549–1611), chanoine de la basilique de Santa Marie Maggiore à Rome* (Paris: Alain Baudry, 2011).

[14] See the essays collected in Miller, *Peiresc's Orient: Antiquarianism as Cultural History in the Seventeenth Century* (Farnham: Ashgate, 2012).

[15] This is the subject of my forthcoming *Peiresc and the Mediterranean*.

[16] For his work on the nature and natural history of the Mediterranean, see Miller, "Peiresc and the First Natural History of the Mediterranean," *Sintflut und Gedächtnis*, Jan Assman and Martin Mulsow, eds. (Paderborn: Wilhelm Fink Verlag, 2006), 167–198; and idem, "Mapping Peiresc's Mediterranean: Geography and Astronomy, 1610–1636," *Communicating Observations in Early Modern Letters, 1500–1575. Epistolography and Epistemology in the Age of the Scientific Revolution*, Dirk van Miert, ed. (Oxford: Warburg Institute Colloquia, 2012).

II

Antiquarianism as
an Archival "Science"

❧

ONE OF PEIRESC'S FOUR GREAT projects, according to his biographer, Pierre Gassendi, was a *History of Provence* (the others were studies of the Calendar of 354 CE, of the newly discovered moons of Jupiter, and of ancient vases). Of them all, a *History of Provence* is the one that lets us penetrate most deeply into Peiresc's practice of historical research. Peiresc's close friend and collaborator, as well as biographer, Pierre Gassendi, described the project this way:

> To that end, he took so much care—and what did he not do?—in order to pull out a history from the ashes and dust of our Counts and give light to its most noble families using to this end not bare tradition, slight arguments, uncertain authorities, but authentic records, such as wills, marriage contracts, transactions of business, law-deeds, privileges and also statues, tombs, inscriptions, pictures, scutcheons, coins, seals and other things of this sort. Which, that he might discover and get into his hands, he spared no cost, effort or industry; perusing himself, or causing to be perused, all acts and monuments which could be found in the treasuries and records of the princes, bishops, abbots, chapters, monasteries, nunneries, nobles, gentry, and private persons whomsoever. Also in the statutes of churches, their registers of burials, and calendars. Causing to be sketched whatever thing of great antiquity, was shadowed, portrayed, engraved, or expressed in books, clothing, glass windows, and buildings, whether sacred or profane.[1]

Gassendi's description reads like a "perfect," or "total," history built from material evidence. And yet, when a finished and long-lost manuscript entitled *Abridged History of Provence* was discovered a few years ago, Peiresc's practice looked very different.[2] For the *Abridged History* reads like a medieval annal or chronicle, beginning at the beginning and marching relentlessly through time, marking its passage by ruler and regime change—in short, lacking precisely the "interpretative" element that has long been identified with "history."[3] The finished product seems to bear no resemblance to the avant-garde project sketched out by Gassendi.[4] The promise of a "new kind of history" vanishes amid the detritus of yet another unfinished antiquarian compilation.[5]

Had the *Abridged History* never been published, Gassendi's few readers could have consoled themselves with the word-portrait of an extraordinary-sounding project. But since it does exist in a finished form, we are confronted with a puzzle: Why is Gassendi's rendering of the project so much more exciting than Peiresc's?[6] It cannot be out of ignorance, as he knew the Peiresc archive as well as anyone could, having spent the two years after Peiresc's death sitting in Aix and reading through it before writing his *Life of the Illustrious Man, Nicolas Claude Fabri de Peiresc, Senator of Aix* (*Viri Illustris Nicolai Claudii Fabricii de Peiresc Senatoris Aquisextiensis*; 1641). A younger protégé of Peiresc's, Honoré Bouche, asked much the same question. He doubted Gassendi's claim that Peiresc had worked on a big historical project because otherwise "he would not have stopped, for fear of lack of time, at the vast and exact research of such local matters"—the history of Provençal families.[7]

It is in Peiresc's papers that we find the solution to our puzzle. What we discover is that every aspect of Peiresc's study of Provence mentioned by Gassendi is, in fact, found in the archive. Across thousands of pages, filling hundreds of dossiers, are the records of Peiresc's close encounter with documents, coins, inscriptions, seals, genealogies and heraldry, whether on paper, parchment, stone, metal or glass, and whether preserved in royal, local, noble or monastic archives.

Of course, memoranda, reading notes, excerpts of public instruments, essay fragments, drafts, and treatise-like letters are not what we generally mean by "history."[8] Herein lies the challenge posed by his work: an intense historical sensibility, a powerful ability to extract information about the past from surviving materials, and a willingness to entertain potentially fruitful conjectures that is not brought together in an extended narrative. For we see that when he does craft such a narrative, as in the *History of Provence*, it keeps all this intelligence invisible, as if respecting very strict generic conventions.[9] What does this tell us?

It is possible to see this practice as a demonstration of a fundamental split between the antiquary who collects and the historian who writes, with all its implied hierarchy.[10] Yet, stepping back and viewing Peiresc's work on medieval Provence from a distance, the two parts look complementary. Turning from the annalistic *History* to those rich and diverse research materials, we might want to consider them not in Bacon's categories of "history unfinished" or "history defaced,"[11] but as an example of how to "do" history, of historical scholarship, if not exactly "History."[12] If we follow the implications of this, it means evaluating Peiresc the historian not in terms of "histories" written, but of research undertaken; not, in sum, as an author of books, but of an archive.

Archives, as we have come to understand them since the nineteenth century, are the residue of intention, the often accidental survival, in often accidental shape, of past life preserved in words.[13] We tend not to view a scholar's working papers as the goal of his work, but rather as preparatory material for it. But papyrologists, for example, take a different view. They use "archive" in a self-conscious and distinctive way to include private materials, compiled by ordinary people, as well as public documents. "Archive" refers explicitly to documentary, rather than literary materials—for these latter the term "library" is reserved—and can include letters, notes, lists, and memoranda.[14] Peiresc's "paperware," similarly, an intellectual operation made through excerpting, copying, borrowing, and compiling, expresses his intentions. And though there have been some losses over the years, the archive is more or less as complete as it was at his death in 1637.[15]

The greatest historian of that early modern Mediterranean world preserved in the Peiresc archive was, of course, Fernand Braudel. Jacques Rancière has brilliantly analyzed Braudel's presentation of the death of Philip II. For him, it captures the extreme tension between the historical actor and the historian: the one oblivious to the real significance of his own actions, the other with all the riches of many archives at his disposal.[16] The situation of Peiresc and his historian is different. Because of his self-archiving practice, and because he wrote about the historical Mediterranean and acted on the contemporary one, one could unironically write about "The Mediterranean and the Mediterranean World in the Age of Peiresc."[17] Living by the sea and working closely with the merchants of Marseille — both Peiresc's brother and his banker served at various times as Viguier, a ceremonial officer, of Marseille[18] — Peiresc came quite naturally to incorporate the sea and the life associated with the sea into his scholarship.[19] We can know what it meant to him, we can use it to reconstruct his world, and we can do this without using our categories of analysis for his world. The survival of this archive enables us to follow Peiresc's exploration of the medieval Mediterranean by looking over his shoulder.

By focusing on Peiresc's archive, we focus on the kinds of questions it allows us to explore. The Peiresc papers are especially vast and rich. But they are not unique. Early modern Europe was awash with antiquaries, and European libraries today are full of their surviving papers, such as the Dupuy, Cotton, and Scaliger manuscripts in Paris, London, and Leiden, respectively. Our explorations in Peiresc's archive are therefore also an attempt to model — or even inspire — similar digs elsewhere.

What is most distinctive about Peiresc's archive is the revelatory quality of what has survived. If others, including Gassendi, lamented the "unfinished" character of an intellectual life, what remains, as if in *statu nascendi*, allows us access to something much more precious than any finished work: the image of a person thinking. With what has survived we can "think with" Peiresc as we move from one question, interest, conjecture, obsession, to another. Through these papers we may, in fact, be able to get closer to Peiresc at work than to any other scholar of his time.

How did his "paperware" work? We can come close to understanding this in Peiresc's own terms by looking at the way Gassendi described Peiresc's archival mechanics in the conclusion of his wonderful biography of 1641. He explains how Peiresc took his notes, organized them and filed them; how he read and annotated; how he wrote and managed his correspondence; and how he collected books and objects and catalogued them.[20] This account corresponds with much of what we have come to know about early modern learned practice through compilations such as Morhof's *Polyhistor* (1688).[21]

But there are aspects of Peiresc's practice that are illuminated most clearly when viewed not from the perspective of *his* time, but of *ours*. This licensing of an ahistorical approach is, I think, justified in two ways. In the case of antiquaries, it follows Momigliano's own genealogical vision of antiquarianism becoming sociology, which even led him to describe sociologists as "armed antiquaries" (*antiquari armati*). By "sociology" Momigliano was generalizing from the German disciplinary experience of the first half of the twentieth century to broader interdisciplinary approaches to historical understanding.[22] And by the end of the second half of that century, from that broader perspective, many of the antiquaries' questions seemed again especially relevant. Second, there is actually a genetic account that can be reconstructed which connects modern and modernist visions of scholarly practice back to early modern practitioners like Peiresc, though obviously it cannot be given here.[23] Not the least value of this inversion of the typical field of vision is that it can help us see persistent patterns of value and shapes of scholarship that we have missed. In other words, what follows may not be as ahistorical as it first seems.

Thinking about Peiresc's archive as "authored," and the practice that this represents is, in fact, one of those approaches that can be clarified by a backward glance from more recent vantage points. We can begin looking by way of Goethe's "Materials for a History of Colour Theory" (Part 3 of the *Farbenlehre*, c. 1810) and Walter Benjamin's *Arcades Project* (*Passagenwerk*, c. 1940).[24] Goethe, in this section of his massive theoretical reconstruction, surveys theories of color from antiquity to his own age. But he stresses the provisional— "materials for"— likening it to the raw materials brought to a building site that then had to be adjusted for use. Goethe explained that having incorporated so many extended excerpts "this volume should become like a kind of archive in which would be deposited all that the most remarkable men who had worked on theories of color had said."[25] The practical utility of book-as-archive, he wrote, was that it made sources available to those who lived far away from decent libraries.

But there was another reason, too. Goethe observed that it was difficult to study the history of scholarship without either including too much detail, and thereby defeating the reader, or including too little, and thereby distorting the source. Moreover, the originality and historicity of an author was always more likely to be conveyed in the author's own words than in those of a mediator. Goethe's example of a heroic resistance to the tendency to put the past into one's own words, and so distort it, is none other than Gassendi, in his biography of Epicurus![26] This project, which Gassendi worked on and discussed with his master, Peiresc, shares its DNA with his biographies of Tycho Brahe and, especially, Peiresc, in which the life of a person provided the armature for an assemblage of documentation.[27] Even retreating from this model seemed to Goethe not enough; to avoid making the project dauntingly huge, he acknowledged omitting some of his reading notes on the history of color theory.[28]

So, we must conclude, Goethe's book-as-archive transcribed less of his research than Peiresc's archive-as-book. Benjamin's *Arcades Project* (*Passagenwerk*) is closer to Peiresc than to Goethe. For Benjamin also created an archive out of excerpta, short essays, notes, and collectanea. The absence of a narrative synthesis has, similarly, led scholars to seek a "lost," or point to a "missing," narrative masterwork. But Benjamin's own theoretical reflections suggest that it was his intention from the start to present the "Archive," with all of its inherent ambiguities, as the historical creation. Indeed, Benjamin, we now know, archived his own life and his own work in just this way; the *Passagenwerk*, rather than a one-off exception reflects instead a basic orientation toward the past. Its publication, from the notes hidden in the Bibliothèque Nationale during the Second World War, may in fact have misled people into thinking of Benjamin as an "author" rather than an "archivist" or "collector."[29]

Similarly, Peiresc's general disinclination to narrative closure may not be a sign of "failure"—no book—but instead signals an awareness on some level of the gap between existing modes of historical writing and their ability to convey the authentic reality of historical evidence. More than half a century ago, Lewis Namier was criticized roundly by Herbert Butterfield and A.J.P. Taylor because he "persistently refuses to provide sustained narrative."[30] Looking back to the political practice of mid-eighteenth-century Britain, Namier saw a landscape as unfamiliar and in need of reconstruction as the Rome of Renaissance antiquaries. And like them he set out "to steep" himself in the details, warning that the reader "must not mind the time spent over details—we distinguish trees by considering their general shape and their characteristic details, for instance, the leaf or the bark; while seemingly more prominent features, such as the circumference, the number of branches, etc. can be safely disregarded, as so many things which lend themselves best to historical narrative." This explicit distinction between what he was doing and "narrative" history is interpreted for us by Momigliano, who identified Namier with precisely the German-style sociology that he saw as the modern descendent of early modern antiquarianism.[31]

Benjamin, it is equally clear, looked to the material remains of the past for inspiration when he wanted to explode the "once upon a time"—and implied "happily ever after"—that underpinned the nineteenth-century historicist project against which he rebelled. Benjamin's emphasis on the way all historical accounts were constructed ironically repolarizes Theodor Mommsen's mockery of the "antiquarische Bauplatz."[32] In the 1970s, Michel de Certeau reclaimed this same vision of historical research as an "immense work site," identifying the "historiographical operation" with the practice of turning the world as given into evidence. "This new cultural distribution is the first task. In reality it consists in *producing* such documents by dint of copying, transcribing, or photographing these objects, simultaneously changing their locus and their status...It forms the 'collection' of documents."[33] Indeed, de Certeau continued, "'Collecting' for a long time actually means manufacturing objects: copying or printing, binding, classifying." The act of collecting, understood in this way, constituted a "gigantic machine."[34]

Peiresc the author of his archive, then, is none other than Peiresc the collector—the "gigantic machine" now housed mostly in the municipal library of Carpentras, France. And de Certeau actually pinpointed the period "from Peiresc to Leibniz" as the threshold separating "curiosity" or research, to use our term for the endless quest of scholars to transform particularity into sources, from the production of self-contained narrative texts.[35] But the new narrative writing nevertheless could not comprehensively obscure its genealogy. "Biographical detail, an aberrant toponymy, a local drop in salary, and so forth: all these forms of exception, symbolized in history by the importance of the proper name, renew the tension between systems of explanation and the always unexplained 'that'."[36]

Peiresc clearly preferred the open-endedness of research to "finished" narrative. And his "collection"—his archive—is, in fact, full of names, just as de Certeau proposed. Practically speaking, names offered the letter-writer not just an address, but also a route. When writing to someone in Lahore, for example, or even Aleppo, distance was translated into discrete stages, at the end of each of which there was a person who received and forwarded on the letter. Each letter itself often contained a description of this itinerary, with the stages marked by the names of the intermediate recipients as by the place names themselves. This would allow the recipient to reconstruct the route of those communications that *failed* to reach their ultimate destination.

Less practically, but perhaps even more meaningfully, names figure so largely in Peiresc's *oeuvre* because he believed recording them was a form of memory work. Writing to the discalced Carmelite Celestin de Ste-Lidiwine (born Pierre Golius) in Aleppo about a local dervish ("drevys") with a large library, Peiresc explained that he "well deserved that his name, his country, and his worthy qualities might not now be forgotten."[37] On the one hand, Peiresc's observation reflects his own sense of the effort that went into blowing even a breath of life into the dry bones of past people; a name allowed for a possibility of distinction denied to the mass of our predecessors. But on the other, one senses also, much as in Proust, for example, whose *oeuvre* offers the best parallel to Peiresc's in this respect, that this sensitivity to the resonance of names reflects a broader vision in which the past is articulated through names and naming.[38] It was Proust who suggested that the attention to names was a manifestation of a fundamental human curiosity.[39] Attention to names, like attention to a lover, and like the historian's passion for evidence—and the comparison is Proust's, not mine—all are fired by an insatiable curiosity.

> But in this strange phase of love, an individual person assumes something so profound that the curiosity he now felt awakening in him concerning the smallest occupations of this woman, was the same curiosity he had once had about History. And all these things that would have shamed him up to now, now seemed to him to be, fully as much as were the deciphering of texts, the weighing of evidence, and the interpretation of old monuments, merely methods of scientific investigation with a real intellectual value and appropriate to a search for truth.[40]

In Peiresc, we see this attention to names "operationalized" in his genealogical work, the history of family descent and relationships.[41] Genealogy was, according to Gassendi, the backbone of his *History of Provence*.[42] Peiresc also applied this collective approach to the study of biologically unrelated individuals, which wasn't what contemporaries understood by "genealogy" and which we now term "prosopography."

Yet the ubiquity of names and naming in Peiresc's historiographical operation—capturing the fact that the Greek prosopos means "face"—suggests that we cannot identify him exclusively with either of these social contexts of the individual. Genealogy embodies many of the distinctive attributes of antiquarian scholarship, namely, that it is intensely source-based and comparative, ranging across varied forms of textual and material evidence to reconstruct a pre-existing reality. Closer inspection of Peiresc's handling of this information shows that the study of individuals in their social context is no static "auxiliary science," but something that points toward a practice more like Namier's "social history."[43]

When, for example, Peiresc looked into the episcopal records of Marseille he saw a history of how people lived:[44]

> I saw in this register of Marseille proof of the wealth of many families acquired by the trade in pelts; that's to say, tanning and furring, in the twelfth, thirteen

19

and following centuries. So that among the aldermen or syndics of Marseille there was always one who was a merchant in tanning. They themselves prepared the skins and sold them far away. Drugs were also in the same centuries a source of great wealth. Drugs and aromatics were sold and made by the same people, and we find in lawyers' notebooks big court cases for which the consultations were entitled *pro nobili aromatorio*. All these opulent merchants established rich foundations of which mention is made in this register of the [cathedral] Chapter of Marseille.[45]

This same talent for seeing social reality in lists of names is on view in Peiresc's treatment of his own family's history. Gassendi, right at the very beginning of his *Life*, notes that a Fabri came from Pisa, went to the Kingdom of Jerusalem, and returned to Provence in the retinue of St Louis in 1254, whose patronage he later secured.[46] This "Hugo" married a local woman and was made governor of Hyeres by Charles I of Anjou. The governor's son became a magistrate of Marseille by Charles II. Another ancestor, who had travelled to the Holy Land, built a hostel for fellow pilgrims.[47] On the annotated family chart drawn up by Peiresc himself we can trace *six* generations of a family's involvement with St Louis, Outremer, the Crusades, the Angevin Empire, and Marseille (Figure 2.1).[48]

Peiresc's practice of genealogical research seems to confirm the recent judgment that

> Genealogy, consequently requires patience and a knowledge of details and it depends on a vast accumulation of source material. Its "cyclopean monuments" are constructed from "discreet and apparently insignificant truths and according to a rigorous method"; they cannot be the product of "large and well-meaning errors." In short, genealogy demands relentless erudition.

The judgment is Michel Foucault's and it is wielded, like de Certeau's, though by way of an analysis of Nietzsche's concept of "genealogy," to ground a new theory of historical practice.[49] As if adrift in the Peiresc archive, Foucault insisted that the "true historical sense"—and like Nietzsche he is attacking "high" narrative history—only "confirms our existence among countless lost events, without a landmark or a point of reference."[50]

The complexity of just such a social, human-scaled vision of the past is reflected in the unique graphic form Peiresc developed for presenting family relations. When contemporaries digested genealogical information visually they sought simplification. His charts, by contrast, stressed complexity: not the top-down arboreal model that clarified descent, but a side-to-side development that mimicked the messiness of social reality.[51] History, on these charts, unfolds

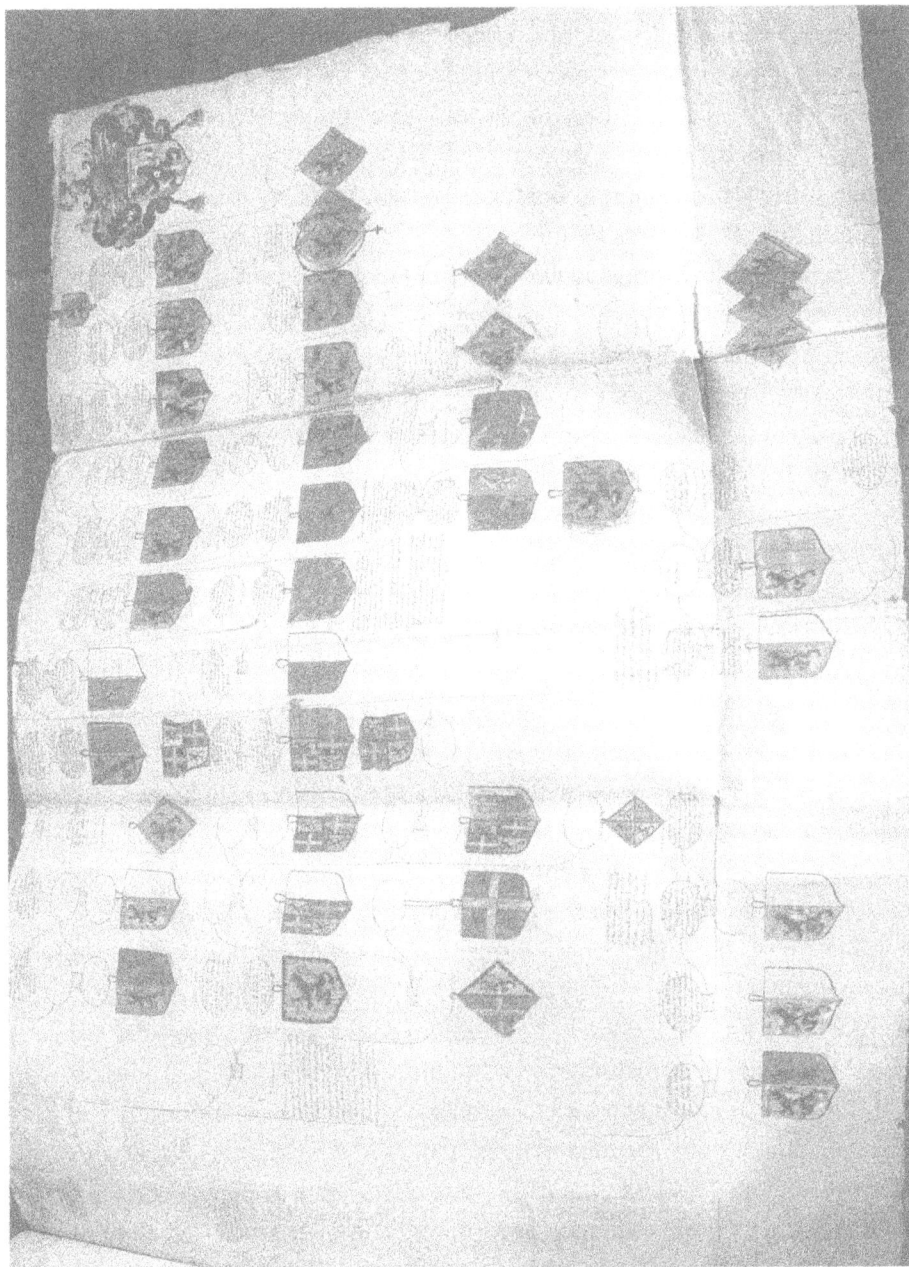

FIGURE 2.1 Peiresc's rendering of his own family chart. Note the biographical details inserted into the roundels representing individual people. The deepest history, and oldest ancestor, is found on the extreme left (c. 1200). Peiresc locates himself on the extreme upper right of the chart, alongside his coat of arms. Carpentras, Bibliothèque Inguimbertine, MS. 1882, fol. 387. Bibliothèque Inguimbertine, Archives et Musées de Carpentras.

from left to right. Compared to Peiresc's organic-looking charts, full with the twists of fate, and weighed down by biographical data, the work of his colleagues appears utterly lifeless (Figures 2.2, 2.3).[52] What Foucault described by way of metaphor—genealogical study of events "not in order to trace the gradual curve of their evolution, but to isolate the different scenes where they engaged in different roles"[53]—Peiresc drew on paper. What Proust saw unfolding in experience—"Thus the empty spaces of my memory were covered by degrees with names which in arranging, composing themselves in relation to one another, in linking themselves to one another by increasingly numerous connections, resembled those finished works of art in which there is not one touch that is isolated"—Peiresc practiced as program.[54] Moreover, Peiresc packed biographical information into his charts, turning what for others was an endpoint, or set of answers, into a research tool that opened up new questions.[55] This was hard work. As Peiresc's friend and collaborator—and the most famous genealogist of the French seventeenth century—André Du Chesne put it. "But how many unknown things are there in genealogies!"

But other forms that captured individual identity while still relating it to a larger family, such as seals, were also intensively studied by Peiresc.[56] We possess an entire volume containing paintings of the seals of Provençal families (Carpentras MS 1784). These were produced to a high aesthetic standard but also with a remarkable aspiration to verisimilitude. Many of these illustrations depict broken and mangled seals (Figure 2.4). Clearly, the charge to the artist was to show things as they were with the idea that even the slightest bit of material should be salvaged and preserved because it could be—or could one day become—evidence. Peiresc's commitment to evidence trumped obvious preferences for pretty things, but the quality of artistic representation of these seals reminds us of the contemporary project of Cassiano dal Pozzo to create a "paper museum."[57]

This problem of nomenclature—how exactly do we describe what Peiresc was doing?—has, as Anthony Grafton and Joanna Weinberg recently pointed out, only become more complicated with our richer understanding of the erudite landscape of early modern Europe, making Momigliano's distinction between the ancient "historian" and the "antiquary" but a special case of a general conundrum.[58] Nevertheless, even posing the question "what kind of history is a history of names?" may help correct two general misapprehensions about the antiquaries' historical practice, and one about our own.[59] First, that antiquarianism, unlike narrative history, was not about people.[60] Second, that what antiquaries produced was synchronic and structural in form, as opposed to narrative history with its relentless diachronicity.[61] Finally, working through

FIGURE 2.2 An example of how Peiresc represented genealogy. Carpentras, Bibliothèque Inguimbertine, MS. 1814, fol. 26v–27r. Bibliothèque Inguimbertine, Archives et Musées de Carpentras.

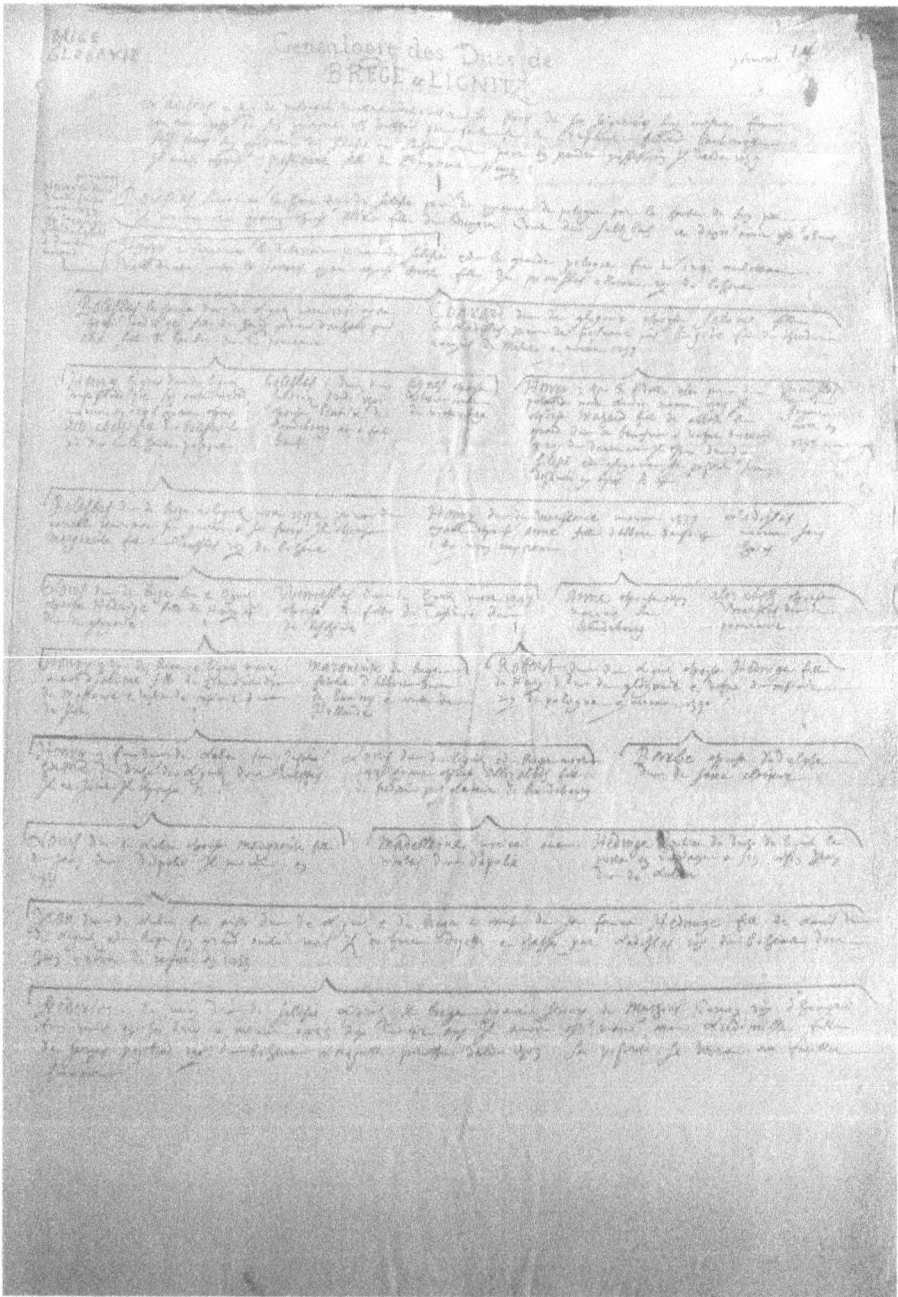

FIGURE 2.3   Genealogical chart of the Dukes of Brieg and Liegnitz by Pierre d'Hozier. Carpentras, Bibliothèque Inguimbertine, MS. 1801, fol. 75r. Bibliothèque Inguimbertine, Archives et Musées de Carpentras.

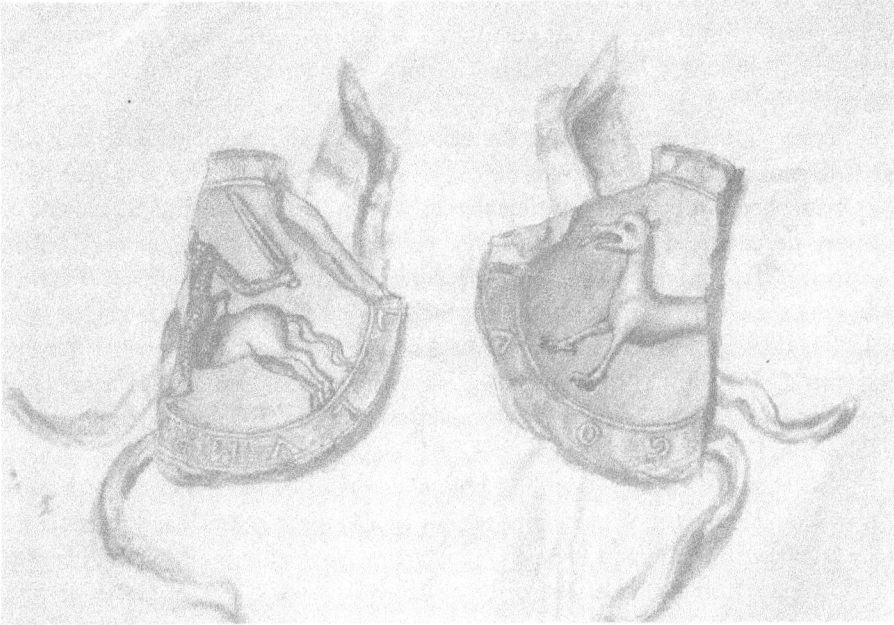

FIGURE 2.4   An example drawn from Peiresc's volume illustrating seals. Carpentras, Bibliothèque Inguimbertine, MS. 1784, fol. 253r, detail. Bibliothèque Inguimbertine, Archives et Musées de Carpentras.

Peiresc's genealogical research shows that what we now call "social history" does not have to be a history of collectives, and that at bottom there is always a human voice, a human face; in short, a name.[62]

Notes

[1] Gassendi, *Viri Illustris Nicolai Claudii Fabricii de Peiresc Senatoris Aquisextiensis Vita, Opera Omnia*, 6 vols. (Lyon: Laurentii Anisson, & Ioan. Bapt. Devenet, 1658), V, 337; Gassendi, *The Mirrour of True Nobility and Gentility* (Haverford, PA: Infinity, 2003 [1657]), bk. 6, 277. (I have lightly modernized Rand's 1657 translation throughout.)

[2] Peiresc, *Histoire Abrégée de Provence & Autres Textes*, Jacques Ferrier and Michel Ceuillas, eds. (Avignon: Aubanel, 1982); Jacques Ferrier, "La Quadruple Odyssée des Comtes de Provence racontée par Peiresc," *Fioretti II. L'été Peiresc* (Avignon: Aubanel, 1988), 305–330. The manuscript of the "Histoire Abrégée" found its way into the collection of Peiresc's friend, Pierre d'Hozier, and thence into that of his son, Charles d'Hozier. When his papers entered the Bibliothèque Nationale in 1902, Peiresc's text was included in MS. Fonds français 32605.

[3] Dionigi Atanagis, *Ragionamento della istoria* (Venice: Nicolini, 1559), most easily found in the *Artis Historicae Penus* (Basel: Petri Pernae, 1579), distinguishes

25

between the narration of events day after day, as in a diary, and history, which "alla narration delle cose fatte aggiunge i consigli & la cagione, perche fur fatte, percioche" quoted in *Theoretiker humanistischer Geschichtsschreibung*, Eckhard Kessler, ed. (Munich: W. Fink, 1971), 66.

[4] Peiresc's table of contents for the volume—since disassembled, with its other contents gone missing—suggests the range of his interests, but gives no clear indication that its method and mode of representation would be any different: "Iugement et Censure de ceux qui ont escrit l'histoire de Provence;" "Traicte des Guerres de Provence"; "Triomphes de la noblesse de Provence contre les infidelles"; "Victoires et triomphes de Charles d'Aniou Roy des Sicilles"; "Histoire de l'Union d'Aix"; "Vie et Gestes de Iean Duc de Calabre et de Lorraine"; "Eloges de plusieurs illustres seigneurs de Provence"; "Remarques des Maisons nobles"; "Armorial de la noblesse de Provence"; "Armorial d'Arles"; "Armorial des Greffiers du Palais"; "Histoire de la Noblesse de Provence." BN. MS. F.fr. 32605, fol. 345.

[5] Nor should we assume that there is an *Unabridged History of Provence* out there somewhere. Although this possibility cannot be dismissed out of hand, there is no trace of any such lost text in Peiresc's 60,000 page *Nachlaß*.

[6] Lest we rush to the easiest of quick conclusions and charge Gassendi with either hagiography or invention, we should remember that he was an extraordinary biographer. One could even argue that when Gassendi thought historically he thought biographically, viz. his *Lives* of Tyco Brahe, Peiresc, and, especially, Epicurus. Daniel Morhof went so far as to proclaim the *Vita Peireskii* the best biography of a scholar written up to that point (*Polyhistor*. Lübeck: Böckmann, 1708 [1688], 239–240).

[7] Honoré Bouche, who wrote in his *La Chorographie ou description de Provence et l'histoire Chronologique du Meme Pays*, 2 vols. Paris: Rollin fils, 1736 [1664]: "Je doute pourtant s'il avoit entrepris de faire l'Histoire generale de Provence. Il y a de l'apparence qu'il s'estoit resolu seulement à la particuliere de ses anciens Comtes, puis qu'il s'attachoit fort à la connoissance des Nobles Familles anciennes & modernes de la Province. S'il eut eu envie de faire un long chemin, & aller bien avant, il ne se fut pas tant arreté, pour la crainte du defaut de temps, à la recherche si ample & si exacte des choses bien proches, & qui ne viennent de gueres loin (sig. biii r)."

[8] Eduard Fueter's massive and seemingly comprehensive history of historical writing had nothing to say about antiquaries as on principle he did not consider erudition ("der gelehrten historischen Forschung") a part of history (*Geschichte der neueren Historiographie*. Munich: Oldenbourg, 1911, v).

[9] Even the one exception to this rule is instructive. Peiresc's only published tract, *Origines Murensis Monasterii* (Spirenberg [Paris]: in Bibliopolio Brucknausenio, 1618), is an anonymous compilation of archival material with slim textual surround. See Miller, "The Ancient Constitution and the Genealogist: Momigliano, Pocock, and Peiresc's *Origines Murensis Monasterii* (1618)," *Republics of Letters: A Journal for the Study of Knowledge, Politics, and the Arts*, 1(1) (May 1, 2009): http://rofl.stanford.edu/node/37.

[10] As in the work of Wolfgang Ernst, for example, "Antiquarianismus und Modernität. Eine historische Verlustbilanz," in Wolfgag Küttler, Jörn Rüsen, and Ernst Schulin eds., *Geschichtsdiskurs* (Frankfurt: Fischer Taschenbuch Verlag, 1994), vol. 2, 136–

147, or idem, *Das Rumoren der Archive. Ordnung aus Unordnung (Internationaler Merve-Diskurs 243)*, (Berlin: Merve Verlag, 2002), but implied also in the dichotomous vision of Paul Hazard, *La Crise de la conscience européenne, 1680–1715* (Paris: A. Fayard, 1961 [1935]), 52–56.

[11] Bacon calls "Memorials" "preparatory history" and divides it into two categories, "commentaries," which are narratives of events, and registers, which "are collections of public acts, as decrees of council, judicial proceedings, declarations and letters of estate, orations, and the like, without a perfect continuance or contexture of the thread of the narration." Antiquities, or "history defaced" or "remanants of history" were gathered "out of monuments, names, words, proverbs, traditions, private records and evidences, fragments of stories, passages of books that concern not story, and the like" — suggesting a greater propinquity to "registers" than "commentaries." Francis Bacon, *Advancement of Learning* (London: Printed for Henrie Tomes, 1605), II (2), 10–11.

[12] This seems also the goal of Jan Marco Sawilla, *Antiquarianismus, Hagiographie und Historie im 17. Jahrhundert. Zum Werk der Bollandisten. Ein wissenschaftshistorischer Versuch* (Tübingen: Niemeyer, 2009), 255, 670; and Völkel, "Historischer Pyrrhonismus und Antiquarismus-Konzeption bei Arnaldo Momigliano," 189, though for different reasons.

[13] See, for instance, the special issue of *Archival Science* edited by Ann Blair and Jennifer S. Milligan devoted to the history of archives (7; 2007), but note that none of the cases examined is adequate to the example of Peiresc, whose archive more resembled a collection than a repository, and whose notion of "utility" was very different from that underpinning institutional archives.

[14] Katelijn Vandorpe, "Archives and Dossiers," *The Oxford Handbook of Papyrology*, Roger S. Bagnall, ed. (Oxford: Oxford University Press, 2009), 217–218; Bernard Palme, "The Range of Documentary Texts: Types and Categories," *The Oxford Handbook of Papyrology*, 363.

[15] Catalogues of the manuscript archive appear in Paris, Bibliothèque Nationale de France (henceforth Paris, B.N.), MS. Dupuy 691, fols. 148–159 (printed in the 1655 Hague edition of Gassendi's *Vita*), and in British Library MS. Sloane 767. Montfaucon later catalogued the material in his *Bibliotheca Bibliothecarum manuscriptorum nova* (Paris: Briasson, 1739), I, 1181–1189. For a judgment see Francis W. Gravit, *The Peiresc Papers* [= *University of Michigan Contributions in Modern Philology* 14] (Ann Arbor: University of Michigan Press, 1950). On "Paperwork" see Ben Kafka, *The Demon of Writing: Powers and Failures of Paperwork* (New York: Zone Books, 2012).

[16] Jacques Rancière, *The Names of History*, Hassan Melehy, trans. (Minneapolis: University of Minnesota Press, 1994 [1992]), 41, 99. He cites Fernand Braudel, *The Mediterranean and the Mediterranean World in the Age of Philip II*, 2 vols. (New York: Harper & Row, 1972), II, 1236.

[17] See Miller, "The Mediterranean and the Mediterranean World in the Age of Peiresc," in *Seas and Peoples: Thalassography & Historiography*, Peter N. Miller, ed. (Ann Arbor: University of Michigan Press, 2012).

[18] For Vallavez, see Bremond to Bremond, 13 May 1633, Carpentras, Bibliothèque Inguimbertine (= henceforth Carp., Bib. Inguimb.), MS 1874, fol. 310bis r; Carp., Bib. Inguimb., MS. 1882, fols. 415r, 419r.

[19] By contrast: "The historian who takes a seat in Philip II's chair and reads his papers finds himself transported into a strange one-dimensional world, a world of strong passions certainly, blind like any other living world, our own included, and unconscious of the deeper realities of history, of the running waters on which our frail barks are tossed like cockle-shells." Braudel, *The Mediterranean*, I, 21.

[20] Gassendi, *Mirrour*, bk. VI, 283–289.

[21] For exemplary treatments see Helmut Zedelmaier and Martin Mulsow, eds., *Die Pratiken der Gelehrsamkeit in der Frühen Neuzeit* (Tubingen: Max Niemeyer, 2001); Ann M. Blair, *Too Much to Know: Managing Scholarly Information before the Modern Age* (New Haven, CT: Yale University Press, 2010).

[22] Momigliano, "Prospettiva 1967 della Storia Graeca," *Quarto contributo alla storia degli studi classici e del mondo antico* (Rome: Edizioni di Storia e Letteratura, 1969), 51.

[23] This is in part the goal of my forthcoming *Cultural History before Burckhardt*.

[24] Goethe is regularly described as a polymath, but rarely is his practice viewed from the perspective of early modern polymathy and its various intellectual commitments; sustaining this argument is of course outside the scope of the present essay. For Benjamin's particular relationship to "antiquarianism" see "Momigliano, Benjamin and Antiquarianism After the Crisis of Historicism," *Momigliano and Antiquarianism*, 348–362.

[25] "Deshalb sollte dieser Band eine Art Archiv werden, in welchem niedergelegt wäre, was die vorzüglichsten Männer, welche sich mit der Farbenlehre befaßt, darüber ausgesprochen." Johann Wolfgang Goethe, *Zur Farbenlehre*, Peter Schmidt, ed. (Münchener Ausgabe, vol. 10) (Munich: C. Hanser Verlag, 1989), 476.

[26] "Der Schriftsteller neight sich zu dieser oder jener Gesinnung; sie wird aber durch seine Individualität, ja oft nur durch den Vortrag, durch die Eigentümlichkeit des Idioms, in welchem er spricht und schreibt, durch die Wendung der Zeit, durch mancherlei Rücksichten modifiziert. Wie wunderbar verhält sich nicht Gassendi zu Epicur!" Goethe, *Zur Farbenlehre*, 476.

[27] For Gassendi's biographical approach, see Lynn Sumida Joy, *Gassendi the Atomist: Advocate of History in an Age of Science* (Cambridge: Cambridge University Press, 1987), chs. 3–4.

[28] Goethe, *Zur Farbenlehre*, 590.

[29] See *Walter Benjamin's Archive. Images, Texts, Signs*, Esther Leslie, trans., Ursula Marx, Gudrun Schwarz, Michael Schwarz, and Erdmut Wizisla, eds. (London: Verso, 2007), esp. chps. 1–4.

[30] Quoted in Siegfried Kracauer, *History. The Last Things Before the Last*. Completed after the author's death by Paul Oskar Kristeller (Markus Wiener, Princeton, Princeton University Press, 1995), 186. Although we might not immediately associate Namier with modernist historiography, the fact is that his "refusal" of narrative reflects a similar rejection of the implied intelligibility of the kind of subject matter that *can be* reduced to narrative form.

[31] Sir Lewis Namier, *The Structure of Politics at the Accession of George III*, 2nd ed. (London: Macmillan, 1957), x; Momigliano, "Lo storicismo nel pensiero contemporaneo" (1961), in *Terzo Contributo alla storia degli studi classici e del mondo antico* (Roma: Edizioni di Storia e Letteratura, 1966), 273–274.

[32] Wilfried Nippel, "Der 'antiquarische Bauplatz'. Theodor Mommsen's 'Römisches Staatsrecht'" in *Theodor Mommsen: Gelehrter, Politiker und Literat*, Josef Wiesehöfer, ed. (Stuttgart: Steiner, 2005), 165–184. Benjamin's view is more famously recapitulated by Michel Foucault in his vision of the document as monument (*Archaeology of Knowledge*. London: Routledge, 2002, 7–11).

[33] Michel de Certeau, *The Writing of History*, Tom Conley, trans. (New York: Columbia University Press, 1988), 72–73.

[34] De Certeau, *The Writing of History*, 73–74. The phrase is Pierre Chaunu's.

[35] De Certeau, *The Writing of History*, 74, 86.

[36] De Certeau, *The Writing of History*, 84.

[37] "[L]equel merite bien que son nom, sa patrie & ses recommandables qualitez ne soient pas desormais ignorées" (Peiresc to Celestin de Ste.-Lidiwine, Carp., Bib. Inguimb., MS. 1873, fol. 404r). In fact, we actually know the man's name: Ahmad b. al-Hajj Husam al-Akalshani [J.J. Witkam, *Inventory of the Oriental Manuscripts of the Library of the University of Leiden*. Leiden: Ter Lugt Press, 2007, vol. 1, 20; idem, *Jacobus Golius (1596–1667) in zijn handschriften*. Leiden: E.J. Brill, 1980], 63.

[38] J. Vendryes, "Marcel Proust et les noms propres," in *Mélanges de philologie et d'histoire littéraire offerts à Edmond Huguet* (Paris: Boivin, 1940), 120. See also *In Search of Lost Time*, vol. 1 of *Swann's Way*, pt. III, 403. (*In Search of Lost Time*, Lydia Davis, trans. London: Allen Lane, 2002.)

[39] "La curiosité amoureuse est comme celle qu'excitent en nous les noms de pays; toujours déçue, elle renaît et reste toujours insatiable" (*Prisonniere*, I, 195) or "Amorous curiosity is like the curiosity aroused in us by the names of places; perpetually disappointed, it revives and remains for ever insatiable" (*In Search of Lost Time*, V: *The Captive, The Fugitive*. London: Chatto & Windus, 1992, 156).

[40] Proust, *In Search of Lost Time*, vol. I, 284.

[41] As, for example, in his work on the House of Habsburg, Carp. MS. 1781, discussed in Miller, "The Ancient Constitution and the Genealogist." That Peiresc did genealogical work has, at least, been acknowledged—in the paragraph devoted to him by Germain Butaud and Valérie Piétri, *Les enjeux de la généalogie (XIIe-XVIIIe siècle): Pouvoir et identié* (Paris: Éditions Autrement-collection "Memoires" n° 125, 2006), 181–182.

[42] "So that it is lesse to be wondered at if no gentleman in Provence was better acquainted with his own noble ancestors than Peireskius was, seeing he examined all their Genealogies, and tryed them by their Records and Coats of Arms, whose variations he exposed, according to the several Houses to which they did belong." Gassendi, *Mirrour*, bk. 6, 277–278; Gassendi, *Opera Omnia*, V, 337. A similar attention to naming in Cervantes's *Don Quijote* emphasizes instead the inherent ambiguity of genealogy (Martin von Koppenfels, "*Renegados, cautivos, tornadizos*: Elements of a Mediterranean Adventure Plot in Cervantes." Paper read to *The Mediterranean: A*

Liquid Space of Architectures, Images, and Things at the Kunsthistorisches Institut in Florence, 9–10 December 2010).

[43] This point is missed even in studies explicitly directed at genealogy and history in seventeenth-century France, viz. Chantal Grell and Mathieu Da Vinha, "Les Généalogistes, le roi et la cour en France, XVIIe–XVIIIe siècles," *Historiographie an europäischen Höfen (16.–18. Jahrhundert)*, Markus Völkel and Arno Strohmeyer, eds. (Berlin: Duncker & Humblot, 2009), 255–274. However, from a theoretical, rather than historical, perspective K.F. Werner has linked modern social science history, under the term *Landesgeschichte*, with medieval prosopography ("L'apport de la prosopographie à l'histoire sociale des élites," in *Family Trees and the Roots of Politics: The Prosopography of Britain and France from the Tenth to the Twelfth Centuries*, K.S.B. Keats-Rohan, ed. Woodbridge: Boydell Press, 1997, 3). For the definition of prosopography employed here, see Claude Nicolet in *Annuaire de l'École pratique des Hautes Études* (1970/71), 297.

[44] A similar approach to similar documents is taken by Martha C. Howell, "Documenting the Ordinary: The *Actes de la Pratique* of Late Medieval Douai," in *Charters, Cartularies, and Archives: The Preservation and Transmission of Documents in the West*, Adam J. Kosto and Anders Winroth, eds. (Toronto: Pontifical Institute of Mediaeval Stuies, 2002), 151–173.

[45] "J'ay veu dans ce registre de Marseille la preuve de la richesse de plusieurs familles acquise par le commerce des peaux, c'est a dire de la tannerie et des fourrures dans les XIIe, XIIIe siecles et suivants. De sorte que parmi les Echevins ou syndics de Marseille y en avoit tousjours un qui estoit commercant en tannerie. Ilz preparoient eux mesmes les peaux et les vendoient au loin. La droguerie a esté encores dans les mesmes siecles une source de grandes richesses. Les drogues et aromates se vendoient et fabriquoient par les mesmes personnes, et nous trouvons dans les livres manuscrits des jurisconsultes de grands procez dont les consultations estoient ainsi intitulées pro nobili aromatorio. Touts ces negociants si opulents faisoint des riches fondations dont est faict mention dans le susdict registre du chapitre de Marseille." Peiresc to Pierre d'Antelmi, 23 February 1632, *Lettres de Peiresc*, Philippe Tamizey de Larroque, ed., 7 vols. (Paris: Imprimerie Nationale, 1888–1898), VII, 74; Aix, Bibliothèque Méjanes (henceforth Aix, Bib. Méjanes), MS. 201 (1019), 71. Peiresc's knowledge of Marseille made him a source for Antoine Ruffi, future historian of Marseille, who in turn acknowledged Peiresc's contributions (Aix, Bib. Méjanes, 211 [1029], Ruffi to Peiresc 17 January 1637, 21 March 1637, 24 March 1637) 161–163. On Ruffi, see Junko Thérèse Takeda, *Between Crown and Commerce: Marseille and the Early Modern Mediterranean* (Baltimore: Johns Hopkins University Press, 2011), 64–69.

[46] This explains his close attention to Pisan and Genoese genealogies. On Pisa see, for example, Peiresc to Gaetano, 6 March 1637, Carp., Bib. Inguimb., MS. 1873, fol. 172v. On Genoa, for example, Peiresc to Boerio, 6 December 1633, Carp., Bib. Inguimb., 1872, fol. 384bis r; R.P. Agostino Schiaffino to Peiresc, 4 January 1634, Paris, B.N., MS. F.fr. 9540, fol. 106r–108v—a fascinating account of histories and chronicles of Genoa—and Peiresc to R.P. Agostino Schiaffino, 31 May 1634, Carp., Bib. Inguimb., 1872, fol. 386r. For the Grimaldi/ Grimaud family, see Peiresc to Luca de' Grimaldi, 18 November 1632, Carp., Bib. Inguimb., MS. 1873, fol. 598r.

[47] Gassendi, *Mirrour*, year 1, p.13; Gassendi, *Opera Omnia*, V, 243.

[48] Generation I: Hugh Fabry, a Pisan, had three sons. Generation II: Jean Fabry, "dit le Pisan oncle de Hugues avec qui il passa outremer avec le comandement de quelque navire" (Carp., Bib. Inguimb., MS. 1882, fol. 387); Generation III: Geoffroy "filz de Pierre Fabry, nommé devant Gentilhomme Chancellier entre les citoyens d'Ieres de l'adveu desquelz les Citoiens de Marseille achepterent Ieres d'Amiel de Fos et de ses enfans avec le Chateau de Breganson au moyen de quoy ceux d'Ieres estoient agregez aux privileges maritimes des Marseillois & en la faculté de la pesche depuis Breganson jusqu'a l'Isle de la Corrente qui est la Tour de Bouq" (Carp., Bib. Inguimb., MS. 1882, fol. 389); Generation IV: "Hugues Fabry conseiller par la mesme traditione fut au passage du Roy St Lous en Terre Ste soubz le comte Charles Ier de Provence avec Jean son frere et Marie de Soleriis sa femme avec son fiz Aycard lors bien Jeane. Et au retour d'oultre mer eu le commandement du Chateau d'Ieres & l'intendance des nouvelles" (Carp., Bib. Inguimb., MS. 1882, fol. 389); Generation V: his son Aycard Fabry "S'il estoit loisible d'alleguer une simple traditive domestique cet Aycard fit le voiage de Tunis soubs le Roy Charles Ier ou mourut le Roy St Louis l'an 1270 en Aout & avoir succedé a Huges son pere tant au commandement du Chateau qu'en l'intendance des fortifications de toute la ville aprez avoir faict on autre voyage d'Oultremer en fort bas age" (Carp., Bib. Inguimb., MS. 1882, fol. 389); Generation VI: Aycard's nephew Guillaume Fabry de Soleriis "fondateur avec patronnage d'un nouvel hospital a Ieres pour les pelerins du St passage d'Outremer...Il estoit homme de lettres fort versé en la philosophie naturelle & avoit faict de grans pelerinages aux guerres d'Oultremer y exerciant les offices de pieté & de charité avec un tel goust qu'il ne voulu pas espargner à l'usage & dotation desdits fondations sa propre maison avec son jardin de toute sa librairie ou le prix d'icelle" (Carp., Bib. Inguimb., MS. 1882, fol. 387). A concise summary of the family genealogy said to be prepared by Peiresc but in a different hand is in Paris, B.N., MS. F.fr. 20262, fol. 1.

[49] Michel Foucault, "Nietzsche, Genealogy, History," in *Language, Counter-Memory, Practice: Selected Essays and Interviews*, D.F. Bouchard, ed. (Ithaca: Cornell University Press, 1977), 140.

[50] Michel Foucault, "Nietzsche, Genealogy, History," 140, 155. Foucault's careful analysis of Nietzsche's changing assessment of antiquarianism (from negative in *The Untimely Meditations* to positive in *Human All Too Human*, once reinterpreted as genealogical) is at 162, 164. This obviously builds on his notion of the "archive" as not an inert repository but a system of multiple possibilities (Foucault, *The Archaeology of Knowledge*, 7, 76, 129).

[51] It is worth noting that graphical forms of genealogical representation are very little studied. Christiane Klapisch-Zuber's outstanding *L'ombre des Ancestres. Essai sur l'imaginaire médiéval de la parenté* (Paris: Fayard, 2000) and heavily illustrated *L'Arbre des familles* (Paris: Éditions de la Martinière, 2003) both focus on vertical arboreal schemes. Pierre Legendre, too, assumes that genealogical representation is arboreal in *L'inestimable objet de la transmission. Étude sur le principe généalogique en Occident* (Paris: Fayard, 1985), 377–384. Nor is Peiresc's approach at all mentioned in Butaud and Piétri, *Les enjeux de la généalogie (XIIe–XVIIIe siècle)*. André Burguière, in a work prepared in Klapisch-Zuber's seminar at the EHESS of 1988–1990, mentions

only in passing an "organigramme," which he explicitly contrasts with the arborial model ("La mémoire familiale du bourgeois gentilhomme: généalogies domestiques en France aux XVIIe et XVIIIe siècles," *Annales* E.S.C., 46 ([1991] 783). Horst Bredekamp's brilliant treatment of Darwin's preference for a coraline over arborial representation of evolution is, however, couched precisely in terms of the former's ability to represent better the inherent instability of life courses over time (*Darwins Korallen. Die frühen Evolutionsdiagramme und die Tradition der Naturgeschichte*. Berlin: Wagenbach, 2005, chp. 2: "Vom Baum zur Koralle," 1837). Mary Bouquet delves into the ontology underpinning the arboreal model but pays no attention to the vine ("Family Trees and Their Affinities: The Visual Imperative of the Genealogical Diagram." *Journal of the Royal Anthropological Institute*, 2, 1996, 60). Daniel Rosenberg and Anthony Grafton do present a few left-to-right "stream of time" charts but do not comment on the different underlying ontologies (*Cartographies of Time: A History of the Timeline*. Princeton: Princeton University Press, 2010, 123, 147). Perhaps Carlo Ginzburg comes closest to evoking the implications of Peiresc's "messiness" in his fusion of visual resemblance and family tree ("Family Resemblances and Family Trees: Two Cognitive Metaphors," *Critical Inquiry*, 30 [2004], 555). Umberto Eco would identify Peiresc's type of genealogical chart, with its rejection of "the rigid form of the tree," as characteristic of a "Baroque mentality" (Umberto Eco, *The Infinity of Lists*. New York: Rizzoli, 2009, 231–233). For a bald enumeration of 7 distinct types of genealogical charts—none of which is exactly Peiresc's—see Johann Georg Fessmaier, *Grundriss der historischen Hilfswissenschaften vorzüglich nach Gatterers Schriften zum akademischen Gebrauche bearbeitet* (Landeshut, 1802), 42–49.

[52] For example, Pierre d'Hozier's genealogy of the Dukes of Brieg & Liegnitz and Brieg & Glogovia (Carp., Bib. Inguimb., MS. 1801, fols. 75r–76v). D'Hozier's printed broadside "Table Genealogique pour montrer la parenté qu'il y a entre Mr le Duc de Lorraine & Mr. le Marquis de Breval" is even more limited, vertical, and abstract (Carp., Bib. Inguimb., MS. 1801, fol. 215v, author's signed presentation copy to "Messieurs Du Puy par l'autheur").

[53] Foucault, "Nietzsche, Genealogy, History," 140.

[54] Marcel Proust, "The Guermantes Way," *The Remembrance of Things Past*, C.K. Scott Moncrieff and Terence Kilmartin, trans. (New York: Vintage, 1982), vol. II, 557.

[55] Du Chesne to Peiresc, 28 February 1632, Carp., Bib. Inguimb., MS. 1771, fol. 228v. Malinowski assesses the genealogical chart in exactly this way: "Its value as an instrument of research consists in that it allows the investigator to put questions which he formulates to himself *in abstracto*, but can put concretely to the native infomant. As a document, its value consists in that it gives a number of authenticated data, presented in their natural grouping" (Bronislaw Malinowski, *Argonauts of the Western Pacific*. Prospect Heights, IL: Waveland Press, 1984, 15).

[56] For a recent introduction to this material that adopts the same approach, see Brigitte Miriam Bedos-Rezak, *When Ego Was Imago: Signs of Identity in the Middle Ages* (Leiden: Brill, 2011).

[57] For Peiresc's commitment to objects of poor workmanship ("si goffa maestria") see Peter N. Miller, "The Antiquary's Art of Comparison: Peiresc and *Abraxas*,"

Philologie und Erkenntnis. Beiträge zu Begriff und Problem frühneuzeitlicher Philologie,
Ralph Häfner, ed. (Tübingen: Niemeyer, 2001), 57–94.

[58] For the problem of nomenclature, see Grafton and Weinberg, "*I have always
loved the Holy Tongue,*" 290. Momigliano's dichotomy is now being challenged; see
Herklotz, "Arnaldo Momigliano's 'Ancient History and the Antiquarian': A Critical
Review," *Momigliano and Antiquarianism,*127–153; Völkel, "Historischer Pyrrhonismus und Antiquarismus-Konzeption bei Arnaldo Momigliano," *Historischer Pyrrhonismus,* 179–190.

[59] Despite its deep engagement with Jäger as historian and geneaologist, the
question is not posed, for instance, in Gregor Rohamnn, '*Eines Erbaren Raths gehor-
samer amptman'. Clemens Jäger und die Geschichtsschreibung des 16. Jahrhunderts*
(Augsburg: Wissner, 2001).

[60] For example, in Peiresc's dossier on Marseille we come across an excerpt
documenting a Pierre de Cerveris buying half a windmill from Jean, Jehannet, and
Samsette Pascal in 1390; a Bertrand d'Agout of Marseille conveying the Chateau of
Cabries to Olivier d'Agout, his brother, and to Bertrand, his nephew, a house in the
part of Marseille "long called" Jerusalem; and the commune of Sixfours purchasing
the right to make olive oil on property of the abbey of St Victor (Carp., Bib. Inguimb.,
MS. 1853, fols. 123r; 125r; 124r). These examples could be multiplied many times
over. Although students of early modern epigraphy from Momigliano onward have
made the connection between inscriptions and the history of institutions, careful
reading of the Smetius-Lipsius or Scaliger-Gruter syllogae shows that names were
everywhere. (See William Stenhouse, *Reading Inscriptions & Writing Ancient History.
Historical Scholarship in the Late Renaissance.* London: Institute of Classical Studies,
University of London School of Advanced Study, 2005, esp. 149–160.) I thank Tony
Grafton for insisting on this point.

[61] Peiresc's genealogical "focus" made him especially attentive to the power of
lists, which mimicked continuity over time. This is where chronology could blur into
genealogy, as in lists of the bishops of Marseille and Aix from late antiquity to the
sixteenth century (Carp., Bib. Inguimb., MS. 1855, fol. 355r; MS. 1857, fols. 1–8;
MS. 1859, fols. 10–13). This same approach could also underpin the study of political
units: viz. for Aquitaine (Carp., Bib. Inguimb., MS. 1792, fol. 178bis), Rome (fol. 180),
Provence (fol. 182), Norsemen (fols. 184–185), Saxons (fol. 190), "Alamannorum" (fol.
192).

[62] It has long been noted that early modern antiquaries devoted a great deal of
attention to etymology. This suggests an awareness of the singularity of names and
naming that could spill over into nonetymological pursuits. See, for example, Linda
Van Norden, "Peiresc and the English Scholars," *Huntington Library Quarterly,* 12
(1949), 377–378.

III

Researching the *History* of Provence

❧

TURNING NOW TO PEIRESC'S HISTORY of medieval Provence, it is not surprising that he would see it as a family history—or a history of families. But he was also working precisely at a moment when the genealogy of nobility became a matter of concern for both rulers and ruled.[1] That he chose to frame this *History of Provence* as a Mediterranean history tells us something about how Peiresc thought the different strata of his archive best fit together.

In Carpentras, 10 volumes survive that are devoted specifically to different families (as many, in fact, as are devoted to his correspondence).[2] They contain a variety of information, ranging from excerpts of birth, baptismal, marriage, and death documents, many of which bear notarial attestations of accuracy, to criminal proceedings and royal declarations. Family charts in one or another state of completion are typical. So are depictions and descriptions of seals and the iconography of funerary monuments. Peiresc sought out the same kinds of information for the ruled as for the rulers. Nevertheless, that there was so much more material available for documenting the Counts of Barcelona–Provence or the Angevin kings meant that Peiresc could range widely and deeply in his pursuit of their pasts. Peiresc's interest in the Middle Ages was part of a turn already evident in the previous generation.[3]

Establishing an accurate history of Provence meant, so it might seem to a reader of Peiresc's *History*, clarifying basic facts of rulers, reigns, and events. This, however, was not so simple. Peiresc's tangled genealogical charts convey the complexity of the reality he was grappling with (Figures 3.1 and 3.2).[4] But reading through the material assembled by Peiresc shows him alert to, and inquiring deeply into, the full Mediterranean dimensions of this provincial history. For the advent in Provence of the Berenguer Lords of Barcelona in 1112 created a new reality in the Western Mediterranean, whereas the ambitions of their Angevin successors after 1263 turned to the East, and an empire that connected Aix with Naples, Palermo, Albania, Cyprus, Jerusalem, and—almost—Constantinople.

Like many in his local world, the Angevin dynasty represented to Peiresc the "good old days." Characteristically, he studied their material as well as textual traces. He analyzed the coins of Charles I of Anjou, as well as old paintings of the king.[5] He collected and documented traces of the later Angevins in Provence, whether on paper, silver, or glass.[6] But he was also attuned, very early on, to the Mediterranean dimension, and to the social history that always lurks in the shadow of politics. Gassendi tells us that when Peiresc was in Naples, at age 20, he examined Angevin tombs, and noted the presence nearby of Provençal families who chose to follow their fortune to Naples (and were buried there).[7] Over the years that followed, Peiresc acquired what must have been an unrivalled facility with the archival record of the Angevins.[8] Nor did he look in archives for textual documentation only. The materiality of the

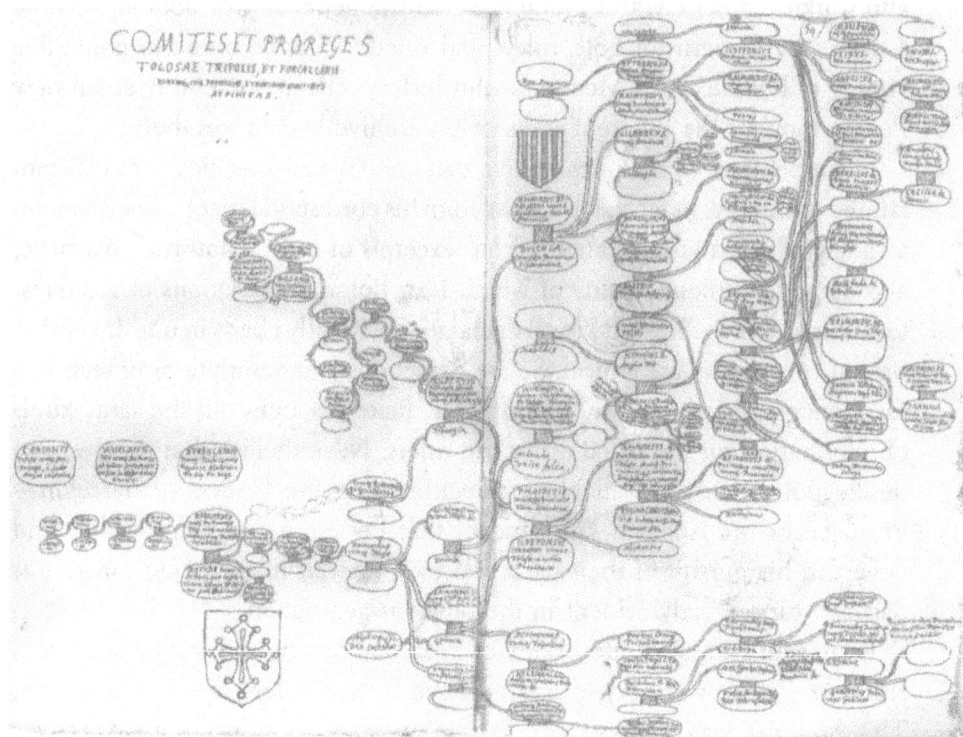

COMITES ET PRORECES
TOLOSAE TRIPOLIS, ET FORCALOBII

FIGURE 3.1   Peiresc's chart of the Counts of Toulouse and Provence (B.N. MS. N.a.f. 5174, fols. 59r–58v). Bibliothèque Nationale, Paris.

document, like that of the physical space of the archive, was noted and treated by Peiresc as potential evidence.[9] This tremendous ease of navigation and sure-handedness with the sources enabled Peiresc to build up, through assiduous excerpting of legal texts, a comprehensive record of Angevin Mediterranean aspirations and also the subsequent French reaction.[10] This material remains essential for studying the history of this region at that time.[11]

In 1630, while trapped in Belgentier by a combination of plague and civil unrest (the "Revolt of the Cascaveau") Peiresc had his bookbinder, Simon Corberan, who remained in Aix, send some of his manuscript books. Near the head of the list we find "Customs of Barcelona's constitution Peace, Treaties & Privileges." Near the middle there is a listing for "marine Consulat routier."[12] These both point to Peiresc's research into the "Llibre del Consolat de Mar," the first postclassical maritime law. He seems to have been its first modern researcher.[13]

This project, in turn, appears to have been driven by a very contemporary need. Responding to an intensified Spanish threat to French coasts, and dissatis-

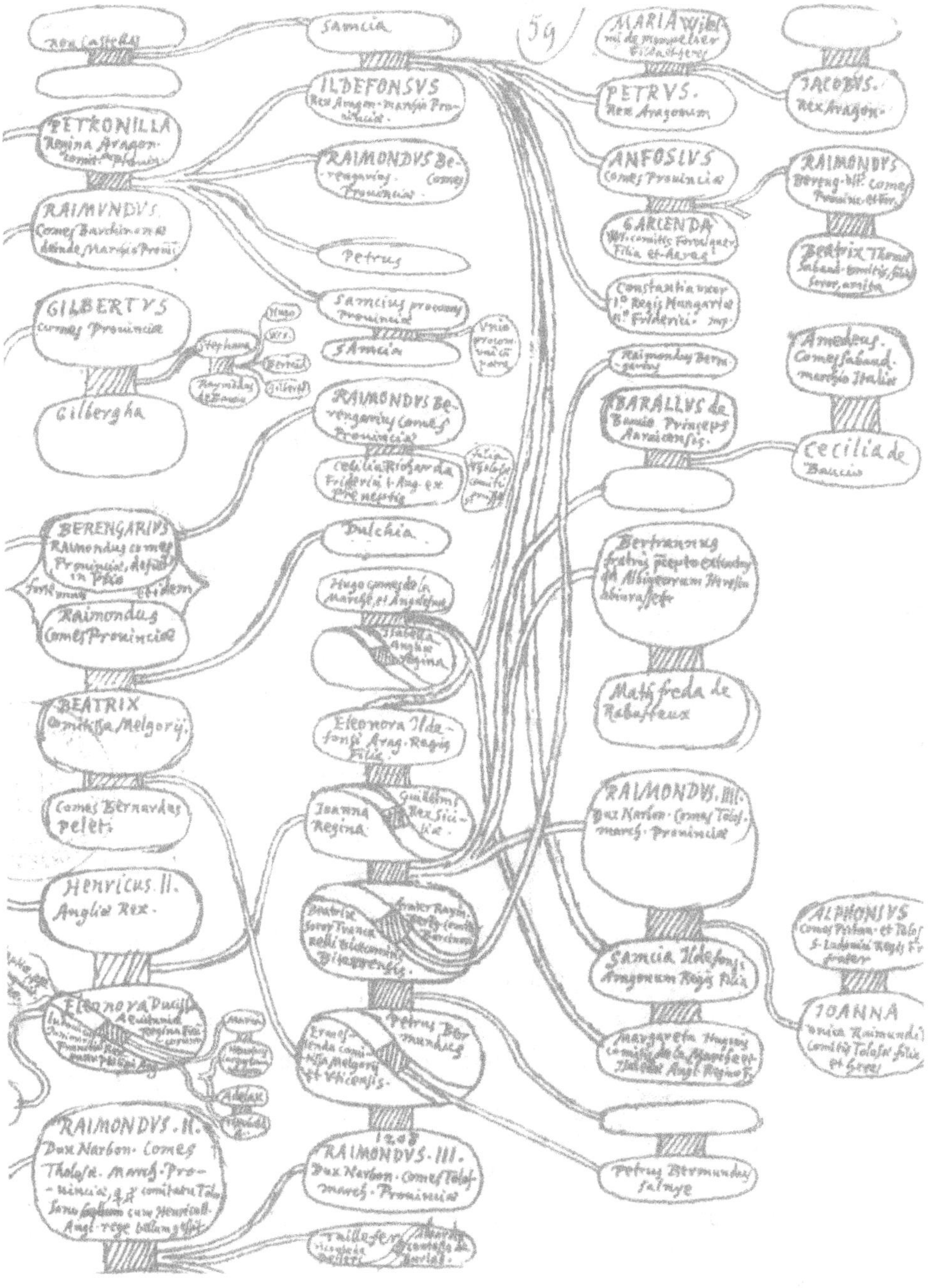

FIGURE 3.2   Peiresc's chart of the Counts and Toulouse and Provence (B.N. MS. N.a.f. 5174, fols. 58v–59r), detail.   Bibliothèque Nationale, Paris.

fied with existing French maritime strategy, Cardinal Richelieu began to mobilize a research team. Echoes of this endeavor filter into the Peiresc correspondence as early as spring 1627.[14] By that summer, Peiresc had been brought into the project, perhaps through his friend and correspondent, the Secretary of State Henri-Auguste de Lomenie. Looking through some of his materials for historical *comparanda*, Peiresc noted that "there was a book commonly found among men concerned with navigation entitled The Book of the *Consulat de la mer*, which is found in French and Italian" and might contain material worth pursuing. Peiresc promised to make "a little tour" in Marseille and explore the archives of the Hotel de Ville, making "the most exact research that I could."[15]

At the end of 1627, Peiresc informed the Dupuy brothers in Paris that his Roman friends, knowing "of the research that I am making of the nautical customs of the coasts of Italy," had informed him that Lucas Holstenius had seen in Robert Cotton's library in London a book made in Pisa four or five hundred years earlier "that described all the coasts of the Mediterranean Sea" and indicated the reach of the local sovereign powers. The particular difficulty of working with Cotton, whose goodwill Peiresc had strained by keeping his late antique illuminated Genesis for years, and the general hostilities between France and England, made it unlikely that the whole book would ever pass over the water, but Peiresc hoped that at least the section on the coast of Provence could be copied.[16] In the first half of 1628 Peiresc wrote to Holstenius and obtained from him a copy of his excerpta of the first few pages of the manuscript known to scholars today as the "Pisan Portulan." It is the oldest surviving portulan text and perfectly complemented Peiresc's simultaneous pursuit of a Mediterranean maritime code.[17]

By January 1628 it was clear to Peiresc that Richelieu's historical interest had a direct practical implication: suppression of the old office of Admiral of the Levant. Indeed, this was the beginning of the trajectory that led to the *Règlement du Roi sur le fait de la Marine* of 21 March 1631 and Richelieu's assumption of the title *grand maître et surintendant de la navigation*. In this redistribution of power, it must be remembered, Peiresc's own brother-in-law, Henri de Seguiran, became the Cardinal-Duke's *lieutenant général en l'intendance de la Marine*, leading to the Seguiran report on the defense of the coasts of Provence of 1633.[18]

In 1629 Peiresc formulated a program for capturing the earliest edition of the *Llibre del Consolat de Mar*: "Memoires and instructions for one doing research on old manuscript books of the *Consulat de la Mer* which could be done in Barcelona."[19] Peiresc began by identifying the content of the book as "concerning the judgment of mercantile affairs and naval warfare." The text had been written in Catalan but then translated into Italian and French. The earliest editions were, however, in Catalan and the oldest was printed in Barcelona in a small quarto in 1523.[20] The book included information on consuls, judges, scriveners, and the making of boats and maritime negotiation. But it was the "privileges and ordinances" that Peiresc termed "possibly the most curious of the whole volume and likely the most ancient, for many reasons that are too long to spell out here."[21]

Peiresc seems to have zeroed in on this section because its seventeen articles spelled out the time and place of the laws' ratification, mapping a new *koiné*, a Mediterranean united by law, but also by the practices and passions of merchants.[22] Over the years, copyists' sloppiness had led to some passages being omitted or transposed and dates corrupted. This was what Peiresc most wanted clarified.[23]

Because the history of this book was so complex Peiresc decided that someone had to go to Barcelona. When confronted with problems of this sort, problems endemic to the philological enterprise, whether textual or material, Peiresc believed in "autopsy": the direct encounter. As he explained to Théodore Godefroy in a letter of August 1633 concerning the problematic dating of an eleventh-century charter from St Victor, resolving this question would have to wait for his next trip to Marseille, where he could examine it "sur les lieux."[24]

When, however, Peiresc had to rely on someone else being the one "on location," he would draw up a memorandum outlining the shape of the project he hoped would be undertaken. We find many of these in the Peiresc archive, and they offer a remarkable "scholar's-eye" view of how to do research. In this case, whoever was to go to Barcelona had

> to inform himself in particular of the officers of the marine in the city of Barcelona, or other persons curious about old books, if there could be found one or more books written by hand, whether on parchment or paper. Or any registers of the said court of the consuls of the sea, or of other tribunals of justice, or indeed in the Archives of the town hall of Barcelona, in whose registers, or manuscript books, were inserted said laws or customs of the sea.[25]

If his agent were to find the book, he was to identify, first, its order. But "above all it is necessary to search there" ("Sur tout il y fault chercher") to see if the dates of ratification of the seventeen articles were found or not. Peiresc was especially keen to know if the fifth article, concerning its ratification in Marseille, could be found. And if it were found, Peiresc wanted an exact transcription made, sparing no detail of its presentation: "It is necessary to collate them exactly, word for word and letter for letter, and to mark in the margin of the enclosed copy all the diverse readings and differences that are recognized there, whether of letters and numbers or of proper names, or of the other words of the said articles when it would even seem that there was some inexactness, in order to give a foundation to those conjectures that could resolve them."[26] If a printed edition of the *Llibre del Consolat* older than 1523, or a manuscript version, could be found at a decent price, and with those 17 articles intact— that would be all the better.[27] Peiresc even arranged for a line of credit, to ensure that his agent would be able to stay as long as was necessary to achieve these goals.[28]

Peiresc then found someone going to Barcelona: the Provincial of the Minims in Provence, Jean François, who was off to visit the local chapter in the late spring of 1629.[29] Peiresc seized the occasion, equipping him with a detailed set of instructions that extended beyond the *Consolat de Mar* to other problems in Provençal–Catalan history.[30] In this memo Peiresc spelled out something close to the "theory" of material culture that Gassendi attributed to him for the *History of Provence*.

Peiresc indicated *who* he was most interested in—Alfonso I of Provence and Barcelona (Alfonso II of Aragon), called "the Chaste" (1157–1196) and his wife; his father, Raimon Berenguer IV (1113–1162); his mother, Queen Petronilla (1135–1174); his grandfather, Ramon Berenguer III (1082–1131); and, above all, his grandmother, the Countess Dulcia (1095–1190)—but also *what* he most wanted. He was quite specific about his desire for material and iconographic traces. First of all, he spoke of seals. He wanted charters "where the old seals were attached, to take down the most exact possible description of them. . . . And if one could make a mold of them and take the impressions, at least of the face, that would be very curious."[31] Peiresc's evidentiary imagination is fully on display here, just as Gassendi had asserted in his biography. For, Peiresc continued, turning from seals to other kinds of material culture, "If there are statues or paintings of those princes, on the gates, in the windows, on the altars or reliquaries, chalices, Cross and other instruments of the church, one could also remark on them."[32] After doing this at the Benedictine monastery of S. Maria de Ripoll—an ancient dependent of St Victor of Marseille—Peiresc suggested the Minim do the same at the Cistercian monastery of Poblet, which he estimated as no more distant from Barcelona.

Although Peiresc's research into medieval maritime law may have been driven by some present need, his other focus, on the Counts of Barcelona–

Provence was a much older concern. Indeed, the attention to iconographical clarity here reprises the import of a set of instructions Peiresc had fashioned for his factotum, Denis Guillemin, in June 1609, when sending him to Angers to discover and describe in writing whatever tombs could be located of the Counts of Provence and Dukes of Anjou. Peiresc had asked him "to make in color, or in pencil on paper of the same size as this leaf, the figures of the said counts or countesses, except for King René, who is well-known to us. And that the figures should all be in full, with the true way of their clothes, just as one finds them." While in the area, he was to examine nearby monasteries for new material and "to mark well the places where they are found."[33]

In 1626, when Cardinal Francesco Barberini passed from Provence to Spain as Papal Legate, Peiresc charged him with a range of archival tasks. We know this because Peiresc's letter thanking the Cardinal for three inscriptions mentions also that in the archives of the monastery of Poblet he hoped to find cartularies "in which, I have no doubt there won't be found seals where their figures are represented, with the clothing or weapons used in those times."[34]

Three years later, Peiresc directed his agent to the paintings of the Counts and Kings of Aragon in the House of the Deputation (*Diputació*) in the city of Barcelona, but warned "that these were made at whim, without any relationship to their true portraits, nor to the costume of their time." There were similarly ahistorical depictions in the tomb sculptures of the cathedral. But if there were any authentic portraits of Alfonso the Chaste or of his grandmother Dulcia, Peiresc wanted a sketch. Peiresc recalled that he had tried to program Cardinal Francesco Barberini "to do a little bit of research on these portraits" during his legation, but that he had fallen ill and those whom he employed simply went to the Deputation and fell for the fakes.[35]

But how to ensure that the Minim did not make the same mistake as Francesco Barberini's helpers? Peiresc is here trying to remotely pilot the connoisseurship of portrait styles of medieval Provence—Catalonia—not an area where he could naturally count on his agent's skill. So, as was the case with his memoires to Levant-bound travellers, Peiresc spelled out as much as possible the thinking behind his criteria of judgment. And the really interesting thing here, suggesting that the study of antiquities was the foundation for his medieval studies, is the role of numismatic portraiture as the baseline of veracity. "In order to really recognize if the manner of the portraits that one will find there will correspond to the antique manner, of the time of that prince, there is added to this memoire a couple of small silver monies struck in Provence on the authority of that King Alfonso the Chaste, while he possessed the sovereignty."[36]

Nevertheless, coins alone could not suffice. For although they were precise indicators of material culture—they permitted clothes, hairstyle, crowns, beards to be dated—their small size limited their utility for identifying people:

> ... and for judging if there is a relationship of the ones [sculptures] to the others [coins] since if it isn't found there, it is an incontrovertible point that the portraits are not faithful, since the money of the times can not be thrown in doubt because of the [contemporaneity of] the clothing or crowns and of wearing a beard or not. But as for the resemblance of the face, the smallness of the monies does not allow for them to be exactly observed by the crude workers such as those of that time.[37]

Therefore, Peiresc, continued, it was necessary to pursue this comparison across the range of material culture: "in order to compare the portrait of that Prince (who is there represented clean-shaven, having a simple and large crown) with the portraits or statues on tombs or church fronts, or on altars, windows, reliquaries, chalices and other church vessels, and other places where such portraits could have been conserved."[38]

If Pere François had the time, Peiresc suggested that he undertake the same comprehensive trawl for evidence through the archives of the Cathedral of Barcelona as he would have at Ripoll and Poblet. But just to make sure he was understood, Peiresc used this as an occasion to repeat his list of possible sources. Again, it is the richness of the evidentiary imagination that is so striking:

> ... for the tombs, epitaphs, sculpted armoiries or portraits of those princes and princesses, made on the doors of churches and chapels, altars, windows, reliquaries, Cross, chalices and other vessels and utensils of the Church. And especially, for the manuscript chronicles, anniversaries, charters and ancient documents, of the seals of King Alfonso the Chaste and of his grandfather and grandmother.[39]

Finally, if the Minim could find some lettered cleric to help him, Peiresc offered to render reciprocal services in Provence, furnishing books and other things "that could serve for the knowledge of their history, just as theirs serves for ours"—Peiresc leaving no doubt that what he was aiming at was "history."[40] Jean François, however, reported great difficulty in finding either a book or a person who could help. He blamed the southern European ways. "Matters go in such slowness in this city, that we were 8 or 10 whole days to find the opening to see the ancient archives and those of the [cathedral] chapter of Barcelona."[41] (Five full years later Peiresc received a "Memoire du Sr Rafael Dominique extrait des archives de Barcellone 25 October 1634." He described himself as archivist—"arxivier"—of the "real arxive de barcelona."[42] He responded to Peiresc's interest in the Countess Dulcia who married the Count of Barcelona and so made him and his heirs into Counts of Provence.[43])

Father Jean François proved more successful with the other part of his charge: locating a copy the *Llibre del Consolat de Mar*. In the Peiresc archive we find an extract referring to precisely the passage in the third part of the book signalled by Peiresc in his instructions.[44] From it we learn that the maritime law was accepted in Rome, 1076 (article 1), in Acre in September 1102, while King and the Count of Toulouse were en route to Jerusalem (article 2).[45] The law was adopted by the Pisans in Mallorca in 1102 (article 3) and in Pisa itself in 1118 (article 4). Article 5, for which Peiresc had explicitly wanted documentation, indicated that the "consulat de la mer" was signed in Marseille in the house of the Hospital during the rule of Sr "Jaufie antox" (Geoffroy Autax) as *podestà*. In 1175 the laws were adopted in Almeira by the Count of Barcelona and by the Genoese (article 6), in 1186 in Genoa itself (article 7), in February 1187 it was signed into law by King William in Brindisi (article 8), in 1190 in Rhodes (article 9), in 1200 by the prince of Morea (article 10), in 1225 by the Venetians in Constantinople in the Hagia Sofia (article 11), and in 1225 by the Count of Germany [sic](article 12). The laws were adopted in Messina in 1225 (article 13); in France, in the presence of the Templars, Hospitallers, and Admiral of the Levant in 1250 (article 14); in Constantinople by the Paleologan Emperor in 1262 (article 15); in 1270, in Syria, by Frederick of Cyprus and in Constantinople by the Emperor Constantine (article 16); and in 1270 by King Jaume of Aragon and Majorca (article 17).[46]

This chronology maps Peiresc's Mediterranean—and the inference from commerce to civilization is Peiresc's. In 1627, at the very beginning of this project, he wrote to the Dupuy brothers expressing his pleasure at Cardinal Richelieu's recognition of their mutual friend Théodore Godefroy's talents, but "especially the work he undertook touching on the treaties made with foreigners concerning commerce." Peiresc hoped that Godefroy, and their other friend, André Du Chesne, would come down and tour the archives in Mediterranean cities such as Montpelier where "they would find treaties made between the consuls of Montpellier and all the greatest powers of the inhabitable lands of 2 or 300 years ago, such as the Emperors of Constantinople, the Venetians, the kings of Naples, Sicily, Cyprus, Spain, England, Scotland, and if I am not mistaken, even the Barbarians. All had no other foundation than commerce."[47]

Peiresc's interest in the fourtenth-century law code, "Assises & bons usages du Roiaume de Hierusalem," shows us where these questions led, and how this legal vision of a Mediterranean unity could encompass Barcelona and Jerusalem, without losing track of the names and fates of individual Provençaux.[48] Peiresc first mentions the code in 1617.[49] The importance of legal authority required the *Assises* to list precisely the barons and knights in their different jurisdictions, such as Jerusalem, Naples, Acre, Tyre, and so on.[50] Exactly ten years later, at the very same time that Peiresc began thinking hard about the *Consolat de Mar*, he received from Pierre and Jacques Dupuy an extract from the *Assises*, which, he wrote, he "had heard much spoken of, but which I have never ever seen." It "grabbed me by the nose like mustard," he wrote, and he resolved then and there to seek out the full text. "I assure you that I will excavate so much," he wrote, "that I will disinter something." Peiresc laid out a plan: he would write not only to Venice, but also to Cardinal Barberini in Rome to see if there were not a copy in the Vatican of the old French version. He would write to Naples and Sicily—maritime extensions of France, after all, under the Angevins. And he would write directly to Cyprus, Jerusalem, and Constantinople."[51]

In a letter of May 1627 to the Dupuy brothers, Peiresc reported that he had sent off the letters to Marseille, Cyprus, and Jerusalem in search of a manuscript copy.[52] In June, Peiresc wrote to Viguier, the Marseille-based French Consul to Syria, and asked if the vice-consul actually resident in Cyprus, Jean-Antoine Spanet (Peiresc sometimes writes "Espannet"), could be approached to seek out things on his behalf. He added that he had sent the specific request ("memoire") to one of Espannet's close friends, the Marseille merchant Leonard Danmartin.[53] In the middle of July, Peiresc had heard back from Rome that Lucas Holstenius had promised to transcribe the French copy of the *Assises* that was in the Vatican Library, and that he and Jean-Marie Suares, Peiresc's creature and the Bishop of Vaison-la-Romaine, and no mean scholar himself, would seek out an able copyist who could cope with its difficult scrawl.[54] The index of chapters arrived from Suares in early September.[55]

In November 1627, in Rome, Girolamo Aleandro weighed in on both the *Assises* and *Consulat de Mar*, which as noted earlier, Peiresc was just then seeking out.[56] Later that month Peiresc could write that he had received good news from Cyprus.[57] Peiresc asked Danmartin to write to Espannet for more information about pricing.[58] In his register of outgoing correspondence Peiresc wrote "CYPRE au Sr Spannet vice consul, pour les Assises & autres MSS."[59] So we know very clearly what it was he was looking for.

What he got, a month later—the letter of November obviously crossing—was something else entirely.[60] In his register he wrote, simply, "Arrivee DES MSS DE CYPRE."[61] In fact, what he had received was one of his greatest catches, the *Eclogues* of Constantine Porphyrogenitus.[62] But in a thank-you note written to Espannet on 13 December 1627, Peiresc spelled out the objects of his continuing interest—indicating that *these* were not among the three books brought him by Danmartin the previous day. In addition to "all sorts of books dealing with laws and history," Peiresc was especially keen on "the maritime laws of the *Consulat de mer* [sic], or more precisely, of the merchants in everything that concerns maritime navigation, and warfare, whether the book is printed in any language, Catalan, French or Italian." At the same time that he tried to launch this line of inquiry he charged Espannet not to neglect in his research "the book of the High Court or Asisses and customs of the Kingdom of Jerusalem." He would take a manuscript copy or the Italian translation printed in Venice in 1535 with the title *"L'alta corte."*[63]

Just a few days later, however, Peiresc wrote in his register of outgoing mail "Arrivee de livre des lignages d'oultre mer."[64] This text was produced in the same Cypriot circle as the fourteenth-century version of the *Assises*, but came from Rome, not Cyprus, along with a copy of the first three chapters of the *Assises*. On 26 May 1628 Peiresc noted the arrival in Aix of a copy of the complete Vatican version of the *Assises of Jerusalem*, sent to him by Aubery from Rome.[65] Even though Peiresc had succeeded in getting a copy of the *Assises*, and an excerpt from Cotton's Portulan from London via Rome, and a copy of the *Llibre del Consolat de Mar* from Barcelona a couple of years later, he did not cease seeking variant manuscript versions of each of these from Cyprus.[66]

It so happened that the copy of the *Assises* which Peiresc obtained from Rome included a longer version of the "Libvre des Lignages d'Outremer" than was found in other copies of the *Assises*.[67] Even a brief perusal showed him that his genealogically inclined colleagues Godefroy, Du Chense, and the brothers de Ste Marthe would "find there much pasture for their taste."[68] Peiresc was intrigued enough to tell a new correspondent in Sidon that he had just recovered a genealogy of the families of the Kingdom of Jerusalem but was still looking for additional proofs that could be found in the East.[69] The *Lignages* begins with a defense of naming as a bulwark against the oblivion of eating time, and then proceeds to narrate successive lineages, which together make a thick prosopographical web.[70] Indeed, one could argue that the texture of this document was entirely woven of names.[71] It is, in short, a genealogical view of the inhabitants of the Kingdom of Jerusalem at a moment in time.

In 1635, in Aix, the printer Estienne David brought out a French translation of the *Consolat*, explaining that the book "fell into his hands these past years." One suspects that Peiresc had to have been the one who put it there.[72] Even afterward, Peiresc remained engaged by the chase, asking the Benedictine Father and famed manuscript hunter, Constantino Gaetano (1568–1650), if he had ever come across a manuscript of the "Consulato di Mare" either in French, Catalan, or Provençal. And while he was asking, Peiresc also wondered if there existed any documentation in Rome of ancient, or just old, maritime laws.[73] Peiresc presented Pisa as "the first among the Christians to make a dent in the maritime empire held by the Sarracens for many years, and to seize a good part of it."[74] Gaetano, in turn, cited this part of Peiresc's letter as the sole authority for his claim that maritime law was created by the Pisans.[75] That modern scholars, beginning with Capmany in 1779, have denied the authenticity of the ratification dates found in Peiresc's document takes nothing away from Peiresc's sense of *how* dates of ratification could themselves have defined both a space and a time. Nor does it challenge Peiresc's strategies of authentication—he asked all the right questions.[76]

The *Lignages d'Outremer*, like the *Consolat*, was a book that had a murky post-Peireskian afterlife. Charles du Fresne, the Sieur du Cange, had wanted to prepare an edition of it for publication based on the copy that Peiresc made from his manuscript for Pierre and Jacques Dupuy (Dupuy MS. 652). Because Du Cange used archival sources to corroborate information in the text, had he succeeded in publishing the work before his death he might have been known as the first historian of the Crusades.[77] The prosopography of Crusader families, as studied by the best modern scholars, seems to have followed in the path of Peiresc and Du Cange. Steven Runciman, for example, in *The Families of Outremer* (1959), commented that in the heavily Provençal County of Tripoli, "most of the lords have surnames, such as Dorel, Porcelet or Mazoir, which are not derived from lordships but suggest a more bourgeois origin."[78] Jean Richard, in turn, also emphasized the Provençal demography of the County of Tripoli—mentioning among the landowners a family named Porcellet.[79]

The Porcellet were among those many Provençal families who sought success in the Holy Land. Though no longer important, and though unrelated to his own family, Peiresc devoted more attention to the Porcellet—2 volumes of documents and excerpts—than to any other family history, including that of the Lords of Baux, for example, or the Villeneuve of Les Arcs.[80] Why he did this we can attempt to answer in a moment.

Peiresc's excerpts reveal Porcellets getting, spending, and laying waste their days.[81] That he chose to pull these data out of the archive shows us Peiresc's priorities: He clearly thought these mundane facts of social life were worth excerpting. The cartularies of the Knights of St John of the Hospital, located in Arles (for the Ferme de St Gilles), documented their land ownership and family relations in the Kingdom of Jerusalem. The excerpta from the archive of the Hospitallers (with some from that of the Templars, as well) show members of many of the same crusading families back in Provence and living their lives—until caught in some moment of legal activity, and then frozen for all time.[82] In these sources Peiresc followed crusading Porcellets to their villages in Galilee and Syria and then back to Provence.[83] As Jean Richard has noted, these Porcellet documents show us family relations, village life, agrarian ways, and feudal institutions.[84] Peiresc had the authenticity of this documentation of purchases, land swaps, donations, confirmations of privilege, marriage contracts, and wills attested by the Arlesian notary Elzias Arfeuille, with finding aids.[85]

What Peiresc's field survey permits—or, at least, points toward—is the reconstruction of a family's history. And almost four hundred years later this is exactly what Martin Aurell has done, going over this same ground—and more—to be able to write a history of the Porcellet family. In this case, the modern familiar practice can help us understand more clearly what was at stake in a premodern, unfamiliar one.[86]

A distinctive feature of Peiresc's field of vision was its wide angle. The Porcellet were a Mediterranean family, and their history, done properly, could only be told in terms of Provence. Beginning in Spain, by the year 1000 there were Porcellets in Provence, by the early twelfth century they were in Genoa, the mid-thirteenth in Lorraine, and the late thirteenth in Naples and Sicily.[87] Peiresc paid close attention to this, even more closely than have modern students of the Porcellet. Family members seem to have been especially active in the service of King Charles I of Anjou.[88] Peiresc tracked the Porcellet through the Provençal archives, and organized others to help him collect material in Genoa, Spain, and Naples.[89]

By far the bulk of the material came to Peiresc from the Angevin archive in Naples. The relocation of the court under Charles I and the establishment there of the Angevin Chancery meant that official documents were to be found in Naples as well as at Aix.[90] In the Royal Archive, Pietro Vincenti, its archivist, identified one "Guglielmus Porcelleto" and discovered that he "and others of the Porcellet family entered the kingdom with Charles Count of Provence who became King of Naples after the victory against Manfred and Conradin." The Provençal Porcellets, in the service of the Angevins, were given land in Italy by Charles I; Guglielmo was raised to the title of counsellor of state and made a baron.[91] Other Porcellets, his heirs of the next generation, held administrative positions in the Terra di Lavoro and one, Rinaldo, served as guardian of the children of King Charles II during the king's imprisonment by the Aragonese.[92]

Vincenti, the archivist, was the author of a manuscript book of Porcellet family history, dated to around 1603.[93] After a brief preface, the body of text paraphrases the event that led to the particular archival mention of a Porcellet, followed by the document's location. Thus, that mention of Guillelmus Porcelletus being granted castles by Charles I is the first entry, identified as "in Registro Signato sic 1271 letra B fol. 187."[94] Extracts from Scipion Ammirato's history of the illustrious families of Naples are included in the "book" as appendices.[95] Immediately following, in Peiresc's dossier, are Vincenti's reading notes on the printed histories of Aragon and Sicily by Ambrosius Morales, Juan de Mariana, Joannes Osorius, Thomas Fazellus, and Hieronimus Curita, each giving the passage and locus where Porcellets are mentioned.[96] While he was at it, Vincenti included a list of the Angevin governors of Naples from 1269 to 1414.[97] Two letters of Mariana to the Bishop of Toul—Jean Porcellet de Maillane—follow, and then one from Vincenti to him, and a fourth from another living Porcellet, Luc Antonio Porcelli, to his distant relative the Bishop of Toul.[98] For this project Vincenti seems to have read systematically through the Angevin archives beginning in the thirteenth century with Charles I[99] and continuing through the reigns of Charles II,[100] King Robert,[101] Charles Duke of Calabria,[102] Queen Joanna,[103] and King Ladislas.[104] From attestations at the end of excerpts we can identify Vincenti as Archivist of the Royal Archive in Naples by 1613 at the latest.[105]

An undated attestation written by the "imperial and apostolic notary" residing in Nancy suggests the hand in all this of the Bishop of Toul.[106] His name figures in several other contemporary documents in Peiresc's archive. Thus, at the top of a page containing information on buying and selling by the medieval Porcellets, Peiresc wrote "Extraict d'un memoire de Mr de Maillane prins a Foz sur les papiers de la maison."[107] Peiresc possessed a copy of *Joannes Porcelletus, Maillanaeus, Barri ducatus mareschalus, Joanni Renato Porcelleto, ex Andrea filio nepoti*, a family history in five chapters.[108] To it was appended lists of families affiliated with the Porcellets,[109] and also excerpts from the archives of Arles, identified by year and cartulary book (for example, "ex Monasterio Montismajoris," "ex Authentico," "Ex Libro nigro," "Ex Libro albo," "De Registro hospitalis S. Joannis Hierosolymitani").[110] In the same hand, we find in this dossier an entire Porcellet biographical dictionary, entitled *Index rerum singularium*, but with no front matter. It is ordered by names of different Porcellets, viz. "Antonella," "Bertrandus" or "Reynaldus" up through "Ugo."[111]

We also find in the archive two printed books, the first an oration delivered by Jean Porcellet de Maillane in the Sistine Chapel on the 1st of January 1606, dedicated to Cardinal Scipion Borghese,[112] and the second an oration celebrating this same Jean Porcellet de Maillane at the University in Pont-a-Mousson, near Toul, in 1604.[113] The panegyric is not in itself terribly interesting. But the pamphlet concludes with an astonishingly long list—for a panegyric—of sources from which "Clarity about the Porcellet family is collected." And on top of that, on closer inspection we find that it corresponds directly to the material preserved in Peiresc's dossier.[114]

All this seems to point toward Jean Porcellet de Maillane, Bishop of Toul. But what is all this material doing in Peiresc's archive? Either Peiresc contacted the Bishop of Toul as part of his own study of the families of medieval Provence *or* the Bishop contacted Peiresc seeking assistance with an independent, parallel project of family glorification. However it began, the two projects converged. So, for instance, Peiresc seems to have made a short list of Provençal archives that could contain Porcellet materials,[115] while also receiving from Nancy a list of documents referring to Provence to which he gave the title, "Extracted from the inventory of titles inventoried at Aix-en-Provence in the year 1301, reposing in the treasury of His Highness in the drawer on Provence at Nancy."[116] The document, written in a secretary's hand but with marginal insertions by Peiresc, concludes with the very Peireskian injunction, "It would be good to research" ("Seroit bon de rechercher"), and continues:

> in the estates and quarterly sessions of the houses of the Kings of Naples and Counts of Provence who are Keepers in the said courts [Chambre des Comptes] of Provence, what conditions the house of Porcellet had there, and particularly from the time of Roy René and King Louis, because in the time of Charles 1 & 2 and Robert and Jeanne we find them in the testimony of chamberlains, councillors, governors of the royal children, squires, governors of the city of Naples, of the Duchy of Adelfi, of the province of Abruzzi.[117]

On pages tracking the Porcellets of Provence Peiresc often inserted the fruits of his research into the barebones outline he seems to have received from the Bishop of Toul. Peiresc's notices included the location of the source, with foliation, and continued in parallel with the text up through the fifteenth century adding 43 new Porcellets to the existing genealogical record![118] A series of fifteenth-century Porcellet marriage contracts allowed Peiresc—these are all autograph excerpta—to pull out the names of individuals, their titles and holdings, as well as the transacted goods and sums.[119] So, too, do the wills, copied out by Peiresc on the subsequent pages.[120] And, of course, Peiresc drew up his genealogical charts.[121]

A key document for understanding the shape of this archive, as well as its chronology, is a letter from the Bishop of Toul to Peiresc, dated 16 June 1614. It thanks Peiresc for the interest he had shown in the family history, promising to send him various materials and ending: "how passionately I am your servant and your brother's." The Bishop presents the latest information—provided him by Vincenti, as we have seen—about the Porcellet barony of Calatafimi and Calatamauri in Sicily. We can hear Peiresc's questions in the Bishop's responses: "For ancient titles"—he would send Peiresc the list of those of his own Abbey of St. Mansuit. "You will have the copy of those that you have marked for me"—indicating that Peiresc had already reviewed and evaluated some of the materials. But aside from the Abbey's records, he had only recent materials "and outside of your proposal"—Peiresc must have asked for really old documents—as his oldest were only 400 years old. "Voilà in short," he concluded, "the report of all that I can tell you about our conversation, for our duty and contentment."[122]

If we want to understand better how—and how much—information flowed back and forth between the Bishop of Toul and Peiresc, we would be hard pressed to find a better nugget of evidence than Peiresc's copy—it is marked on the upper right "double"—of a guide to the "Porcellets of Arles," indicating the locations of instruments mentioning them. These include Montmajour, the Black Register, White Register, register of the Templars, register of the Hospitalers, and "ex Authentico"—the same cartularies sourced in the document produced by the Bishop of Maillane for his nephew![123] These 100 documents, Peiresc notes, were sent to Paris on 10 February 1611. Some twenty additional instruments were sent on 2 September 1611 (Figure 3.3).[124] On the verso is an even more elaborate schedule of documents, their sources, and date of shipment from Paris—Peiresc then being there—and the carrier (Figure 3.4). There are a total of 133 excerpts sent in four different packages on 27 May 1612, 29 October 1612, October 1613, and 10 April 1616—the latter date suggesting a terminus ad quem for the project (the previous latest datable material being a letter from Vincenti of 1613).[125]

The lasting monument to the Porcellet was, however, created not by Peiresc, but by Jacques Callot: his early (c. 1616) engraving of the history of the Porcellets.[126] The print was long thought unique, but the Peiresc archive preserves a second copy, now much battered (Figure 3.5).[127] Working within the convention of a Church facade whose doors were covered by the Porcellet family tree and whose walls were screens on which thirty-three scenes from family history were projected, Callot produced an astounding "as if" multimedia presentation. We can follow the family's movements across time and space, from ninth-century Spain to Provence, Genoa, the Kingdom of Naples, and Lorraine (Figure 3.6).[128] We can see them in the scenes that helped determine the family's history. (The martial imagery, in particular, reminds us of Callot's later work on the miseries of the Thirty Years War.) And we can read about what they were doing in the long captions beneath the pictures.[129]

For this is a *tour de force* of verbal, as well as visual, description.[130] If we look closely at those captions we see something very unusual: there are actual citations by year from archival sources. Some of these are from Provence and came from the royal archive at Aix (Figure 3.7).[131] Other images correspond to documentation which came from Naples but which we find in the Peiresc archive (Figure 3.8), and even to information that could *only* have come from Peiresc, such as "the catalogue of the Bishops of Digne" (Figure 3.9).[132] The program of sources was obviously the work of a serious scholar—though the broadside itself identifies only an "L.P.M.L.M. Collector" alongside of "Jac. Callot sculptor."

The presence of this print in Carpentras alerts us to a possible relationship between Peiresc's research project and the commissioning of Callot. We know from Callot's biography that this print could have been executed as early as 1612 and as late as 1616. Callot was himself a Lorrainer and it is suggested that when he was in Florence in 1612 he could have met up with the Bishop of Toul, Jean Porcellet de Maillane. We do know that in 1616 Callot produced an engraving of a historical scene depicting the Bishop in the miracle of St Mansuit—after whom his Abbey was named.[133] The living Porcellets clearly saw a value in documenting this long and varied past—much as did their contemporaries, the La Trémoïlle family of Thouars, whose descendents, in turn, were the subject of a genealogical conversation staged by Proust.[134]

Peiresc was in close contact with the Bishop of Toul between 1605 and 1620. It is clear that Peiresc was responsible for some of the learning assembled by that "Collector." But how much of the material in Carpentras originated in Peiresc's research, copies of which were then sent to the Bishop of Toul, and how much originated with the Bishop, copies of which were then sent to Peiresc, is hard to determine. Yet, even through the mist of time, we see the convergence between these two projects, one about Provençal families, and the other about a single Provençal family.

Callot's magnificent and rare print, as much as Peiresc's two volumes of notes, opens out onto a medieval Mediterranean stage peopled by individuals in motion, in which Provence played a central role: the rise of the House of Barcelona, the Angevin expansion, and the Crusades.

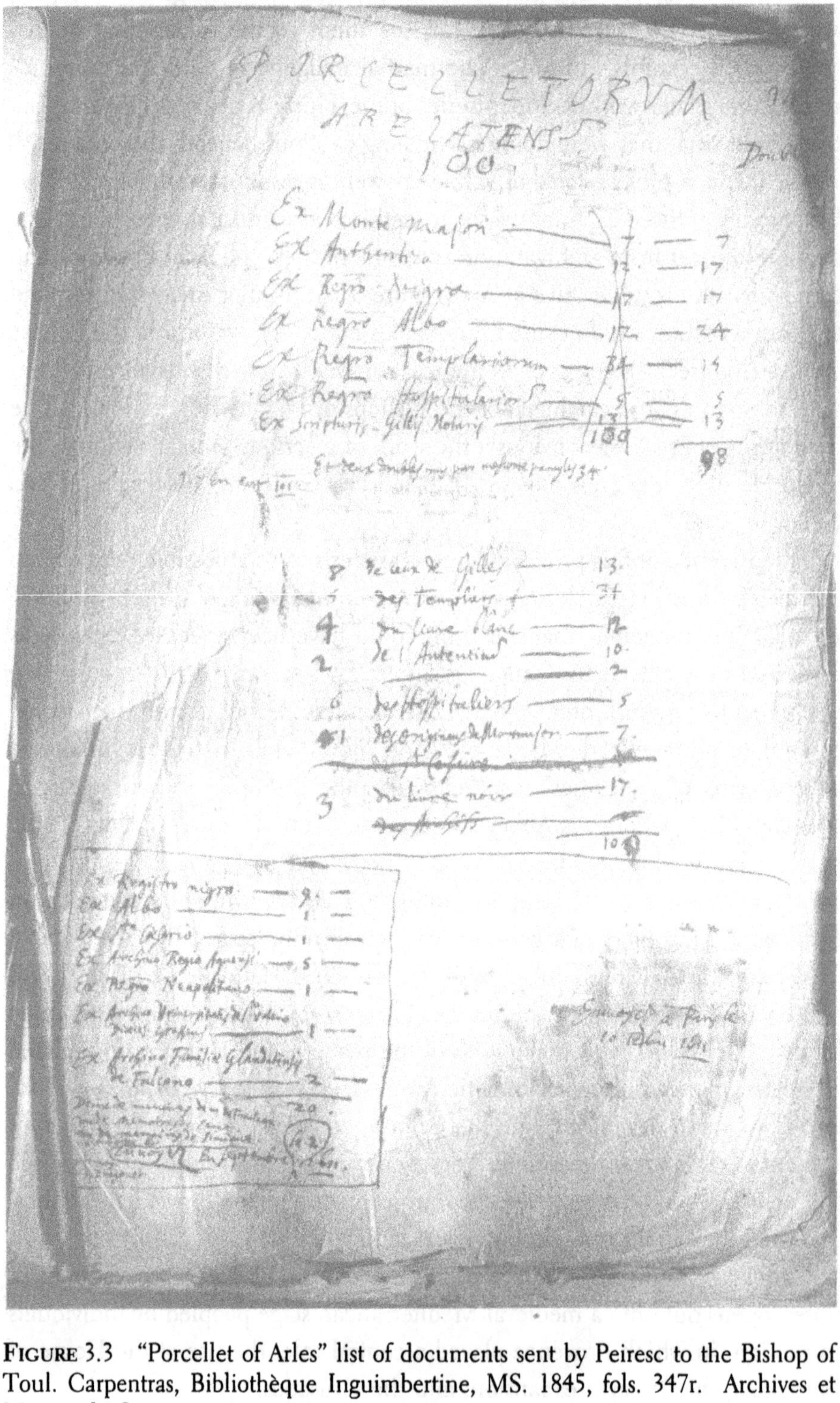

FIGURE 3.3 "Porcellet of Arles" list of documents sent by Peiresc to the Bishop of Toul. Carpentras, Bibliothèque Inguimbertine, MS. 1845, fols. 347r. Archives et Musées de Carpentras.

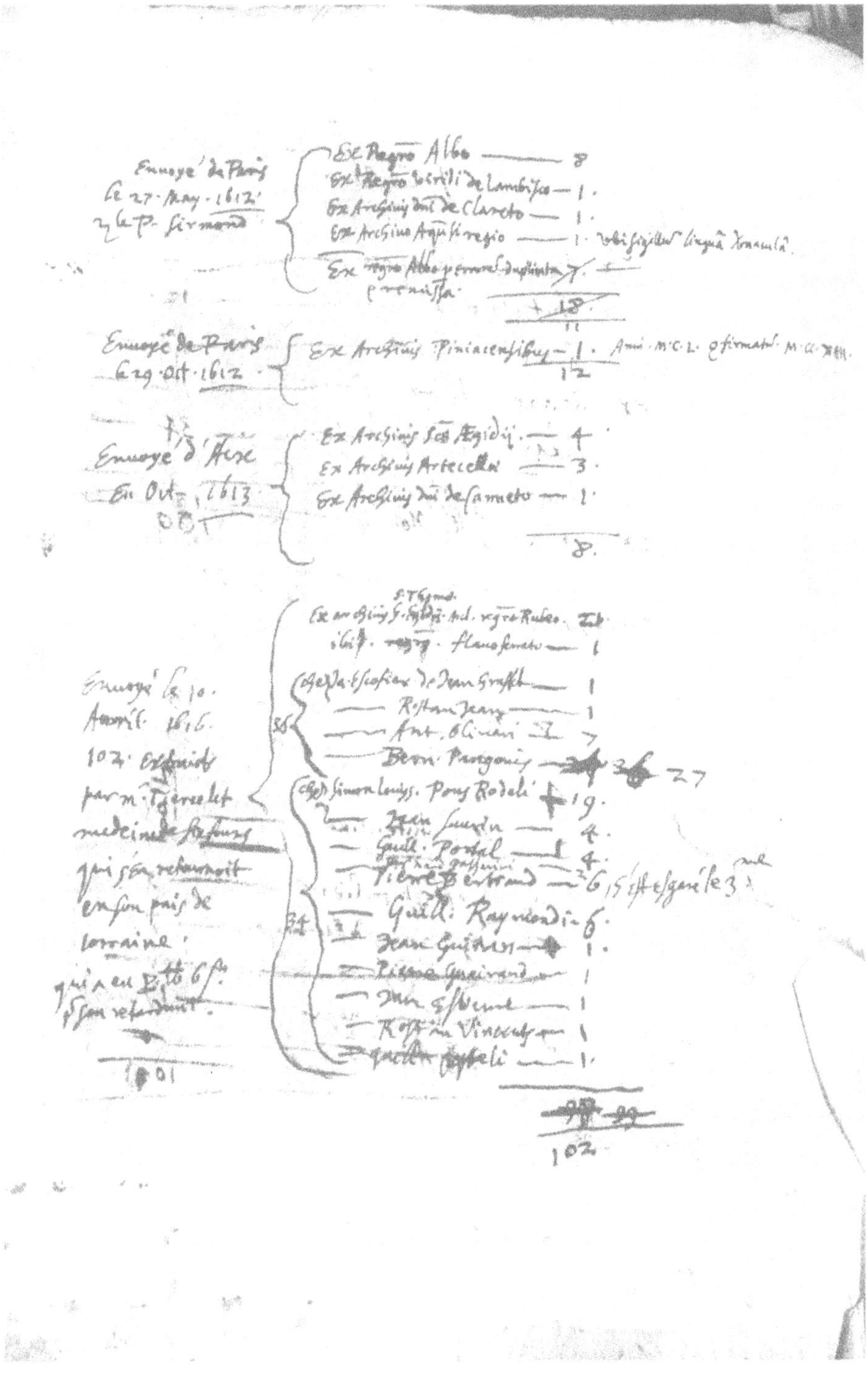

FIGURE 3.4 Continuation of the "Porcellet of Arles" list of documents sent by Peiresc to the Bishop of Toul. Carpentras, Bibliothèque Inguimbertine, MS. 1845, fol. 347v. Archives et Musées de Carpentras.

FIGURE 3.5   Jacques Callot, "Genealogy of the Porcellet Family." Carpentras, Bibliothèque Inguimbertine, MS. 1844, fol. 420ter, general view. Bibliothèque Inguimbertine, Archives et Musées de Carpentras.

FIGURE 3.6(A) Jacques Callot, "Genealogy of the Porcellet Family." Scenes from the Porcellet in Spain. All from Bibliothèque Inguimbertine, Archives et Musées de Carpentras.

FIGURE 3.6(B) Jacques Callot, "Genealogy of the Porcellet Family." Scenes from the Porcellet in Provence.

FIGURE 3.6(C) Jacques Callot, "Genealogy of the Porcellet Family." Scenes from the Porcellet in Genoa. Bibliothèque Inguimbertine, Archives et Musées de Carpentras.

FIGURE 3.6(D) Jacques Callot, "Genealogy of the Porcellet Family." Scenes from the Porcellet in Sicily. Bibliothèque Inguimbertine, Archives et Musées de Carpentras.

FIGURE 3.6(E)   Jacques Callot, "Genealogy of the Porcellet Family." Scenes from the Porcellet in Lorraine. Bibliothèque Inguimbertine, Archives et Musées de Carpentras.

FIGURE 3.7   Jacques Callot, "Genealogy of the Porcellet Family." The Porcellet story from the Royal Archive at Aix-en-Provence. Bibliothèque Inguimbertine, Archives et Musées de Carpentras.

FIGURE 3.8   Jacques Callot, "Genealogy of the Porcellet Family." The Porcellet story from the Archive at Naples. Bibliothèque Inguimbertine, Archives et Musées de Carpentras.

FIGURE 3.9   Jacques Callot, "Genealogy of the Porcellet Family." The Porcellet story from the Cathedral archive at Digne. Bibliothèque Inguimbertine, Archives et Musées de Carpentras.

Notes

[1] Olivier Poncet has noted that "La nouveauté de ce siècle consista plutôt dans la réalisations d'histoires généalogiques de maisons aristocratiques" and sees it as a consequence of royal efforts to fix the juridical quality of the nobility ("L'usage des chartriers seigneuriaux par les érudits et généalogistes en France dans la première moitié du XVIIe siècle," *Défendre ses droits, construire sa mémoire. Les Chartriers seigneuriaux XIIIe–XXIe siècle*, Philippe Contamine and Laurent Vissière, eds. Paris: La Société de l'Histoire de France, 2010, 249). See also, Christian Maurel, "Construction Généalogique et développement de l'état moderne: La Généalogie des Bailleul, *Annales* E.S.C., 46 (1991), 819.

[2] Carp., Bib. Inguimb., MS. 1843: "Traictez génealogiques par l'histoire des comtes de Provence"; 1844: "Titres et mémoires pour la famille des Porcellets, Ie paquet"; 1845: "Titres et mémoires pour la famille des Porcellet. IIe paquet"; 1846: "Généalogie d'Agoult et autres maisons estrangères"; 1847: "Généalogies Pontevez, Rodulf, de Léonne, Benaud, Luynes, de Brianson, de Puget, de Roquebrune, avec leurs preuves"; 1848: "Généalogies Grignan, Simiane, Villeneufve, Sabran, Castellane, avec leurs preuves"; 1849: "Généalogies Sabran, Castellane, avec leurs preuves"; 1850: "Généalogies des Baux, de Foresta, Lascaris, Vintimille, de Calliau, Grasse, Vallavoire, Mondragon, Sceytres, Boucicault, Spinola d'Aix, Clémens, Brancas, Oraison, du Blanc, Laudun, Candolle, Portanier, et leurs preuves"; 1853: "Généalogies diverses antiennes des princes qui ont regne en Provence...Généalogies et tiltres pour les maisons de Bulbone, Requiston, Simonas, Carnuti, Grimault, Flota, de Medullione, de la Garde, Melna, Signa, Revigliase, Jarente, Cossa. Registre de Caradet"; 1854: [Recueil de pièces concernant les familles nobles de Provence].

[3] See, for example, Maria Fubini Leuzzi, "Erudizione, ideologia e politica nel *Trattato della Chiese e Vescovi fiorentini* di Vincenzio Borghini," in *Testi, immagini e filologia nel XVI secolo*, Eliana Carrara and Silvia Ginzburg, eds. (Pisa: Edizioni della Normale, 2007), 461. I do not intend here a more general statement about Peiresc's medieval studies. Nor is this to be found in E.S. Peck, *Peiresc Manuscripts Aiding the Reconstruction of Lost Medieval Monuments*, Harvard University doctoral dissertation (1963) or in Jürgen Voss, *Das Mittelalter im historischen Denkens Frankreich. Untersuchungen zur Geschichte des Mittelalterbegriffes und der Mittelalterbewertung von der zweiten Hälfte des 16. bis zur Mitte des 19. Jahrhunderts* (Munich: W. Fink, 1972), in which Peiresc is mentioned only a handful of times.

[4] Counts of Provence before the advent of the House of Barcelona (fols. 53v–54r, fol. 55r); Counts of Toulouse and Provence (fols. 58v–59r). See also Carp., Bib. Inguimb., MS. 1801, fols. 109v–110r; MS. 1811, fols. 12r–13v, fol. 13v.

[5] Peiresc discussed with Lelio Pasqualini a coin minted in Rome in 1265 in honor of Charles's coronation as King of Naples and simultaneously as Senator of Rome (Peiresc to Pasqualini, 20 December 1609, Montpellier, Bibliotheque de l'Ecole de Medecine MS H.271 vol. I, fol. 16v). A few years later, Peiresc asked Girolamo Aleandro the Younger to procure from Cardinal Farnese a copy of an old painting of the coronation of Charles I, paying especial attention to its colors and to "tutti i diffeti medesimi dell'arte che vi potranno essere, et massime negli habiti, et nelli caratteri

dell'inscrittione che c'è havendo." Peiresc to Aleandro, 29 August 1618, *Corre-spondance de Peiresc & Aleandro. I (1616–1618)*, Jean-François Lhote and Danielle Joyal, eds. (Clermont-Ferrand: Adosa, 1995), 216.

[6] Peiresc preserved a beautifully drawn armoirie of Charles I of Anjou that he found in a book in the house of the Marquis d'Urfé (Carp., Bib. Inguimb., MS. 1771, 283r). In the Church of St. Madeleine in St Maximin, a veritable Angevin shrine, Peiresc documented a reliquary of the Magdalene with an escutcheon of Charles II, a reliquary of the "Ste Ampoulle," made for Roi René, and in the windows of the presbytery escutcheons of Anjou, Jerusalem, Hungary, Calabria, Durazzo, and Taranto (Carp., Bib. Inguimb., MS. 1771, fol. 177).

[7] Gassendi, *Mirrour*, year 1601, 39.

[8] When Peiresc cited the creation of Charles of Anjou as peer of France he writes that it is in "fol viii du registre verd Cotté X. armoire XIII.c xxv bis" (Carp., Bib. Inguimb., MS. 1768, fol. 335r). Peiresc was not unique in this precise wayfinding—when Théodore Godefroy sent Peiresc his own excerpta on the making of Charles of Anjou into a peer, he too, gave the location of the documents ("Registre 1074 de la sixiesme armoire no.102" and "Armoire x registre couvert de verd cotté 1425bis"), though under each of these Peiresc provided his own shelfmarks: "MIL.XXVII six. armoire" and "Armoire XI registre des Testaments XIIIe. xxx." (Carp., Bib. Inguimb., MS. 1768, fol. 336r).

[9] Thus, of a diploma from the court of Manfred, Peiresc noted: "Escript en vieille lettre sur un morceau de papier seellé sur le repli de la lettre en placard d'un grand seel de cire rouge de trois doigts de diametre, mais estant tout fracassé, il n'en restoit que quelques fragments, et entre autres la teste du prince sans barbe, couronné, avec toute la poictrine, et son manteau royal, fort conservé. Dans la Layette Reg[n]um Siciliae, vis a vis de la porte." Carp., Bib. Inguimb., MS. 1798, fols. 640r–v.

[10] Peiresc made a copy of the treaty of Viterbo (1267), which he indexed as "Constantinople, Achaye, Moree" and in the margins referred to the regions under discussion, viz. "Tiers de l'Empire," "Royaulme d'Albanie et de Servie," "Royaulme de Salenique" (Carp., Bib. Inguimb., MS. 1798, fols. 647–649). Peiresc also had copied out the confirmation of this treaty seven years later at Foggia (Carp., Bib. Inguimb., MS. 1798, fol. 655r) and the subsequent agreement of 1281 between Charles of Anjou, Emperor Philippe de Courtenay and Venice securing transport (Carp., Bib. Inguimb., MS. 1798, fol. 658r). Peiresc had a whole cycle of documents from the Latin Kingdom of Constantinople copied out for him (Carp., Bib. Inguimb., MS. 1798, fols. 643r–645v), including copies of imperial signatures (Carp., Bib. Inguimb., MS. 1823, fols. 224r, 225r, 228r). The register of Philip the Fair for the year 1313 tracks Peiresc's detailed probing of this would-be empire's limits (Carp., Bib. Inguimb., MS. 1837, fols. 46r–47v). A rough count shows that 16 of the 42 excerpta concern the Eastern Mediterranean or the Angevins. The revolt of the "Sicilian Vespers" was also documented by Peiresc (Carp., Bib. Inguimb., MS. 1843, fols. 3r–8r; Carp., Bib. Inguimb., MS. 1837, fol. 186r–v).

[11] Thus, a recent discussion (Noël Coulet, "Aix, Capitale de la Provence angevine," *L'Etat Angevin. Pourovir, culture et société enter XIIIe et XIVe siècle*. Rome: Ecole française de Rome, 1998, 318n3) of the decision of Raymond Berenger V to be buried

in the church of the Hospitalers in Aix cites an earlier work (F. Benoit, *Recueil des actes des comtes de Provence appartenant à la maison de Barcelone: Alphonse II et Raymond Bérenger V (1196–1245)*. Monaco-Paris: A. Picard, 1925, 312), which in turn relies on an old source (Antoine Ruffi, *Histoire des comtes de Provence*. Aix: Jean Roize, 1665, 105). Ruffi, as we have seen (chp. 2, note 45) was in Peiresc's circle of Marseille correspondents, and received archival information from him. His book follows directly in Peiresc's footsteps (7–8) but does not mention him (nor does he in the earlier *Histoire de la Ville de Marseille*).

[12] Corberan to Paul, 15 November 1630, Carp., Bib. Inguimb., MS. 1769, fol. 262: *"usatici barchinonae constitutiones cataloniae paces, trezig [sic] & privilegia."* Underlining is Peiresc's here and in all subsequent instances.

[13] Others may have noted its existence, such as Hugo Grotius, who mentions it in *De Jure Belli ac Pacis* (1623) III.1.v, but the more significant discussions are all substantially later: viz. Arnold Vinnius, *Petri Peckii in titt. Dig. & Cod. ad rem nauticam pertinentes, commentarii* (Leiden, 1647); Étienne Cleirac (1583–1657) *Les us et coutumes maritimes* (Bordeaux: Par Iacques Mongiron Millanges, 1661); Du Cange in his *Glossarium ad scriptores mediae et infimae Latinitatis* (Paris: Ludovicum Billaine, 1678) entry, "Consules." See D.A. Azuni, *Droit Maritime de l'Europe*, 2 vols. (Paris: l'Auteur, 1805), and most recently, Julia Schweitzer, *Schiffer und Schiffsmann in den Rôles d'Oléron und im Libre del Consolat de Mar* (Frankfurt: Peter Lang, 2006) esp. 19–22, 28–30.

[14] See Peiresc to Dupuy, 8 April 1627, *Lettres de Peiresc*, I, 196; [?] May 1627, I, 233.

[15] "J'iray voir dans les archives de l'hostel de ville s'il n'y auroit rien de curieux sur ce subject, Dieu aydant, et en feray de touts costez toute la plus exacte recherche que je pourray." Peiresc to Dupuy, 17 July 1627, *Lettres de Peiresc*, I, 296.

[16] Peiresc to Dupuy, 18 December 1627, *Lettres de Peiresc*, I, 454.

[17] Holstenius had himself informed Peiresc of his discovery in Cotton's Library of a text on Mediterranean navigation and nautica. But the accompanying chart was missing and it makes sense that Peiresc would seek it out through his maritime contacts. See Miller, "Mapping Peiresc's Mediterranean"; Patrick Gautier Dalché, *Carte Marine et portulan au XIIe siècle. Le Liber de Existencia Riveriarum et forma maris nostri Mediterranei (Pise, circa 1200)*, (Rome: École française de Rome, 1995), 1–3, 102.

[18] Discussed in Miller, "Mapping Peiresc's Mediterranean."

[19] Carp., Bib. Inguimb., MS. 1775, fol. 3r. "Memoires et Instructions pour ce qui est des recherches des vieux livres MSS du Consulat de la Mer qui se peuvent faire a Barcellone."

[20] Carp., Bib. Inguimb., MS. 1775, fol. 3r; Carp., Bib. Inguimb., MS. 1769, fol. 577r.

[21] Carp., Bib. Inguimb., MS. 1775, fol. 4r.

[22] Carp., Bib. Inguimb., MS. 1775, fols. 4v–5r.

[23] Carp., Bib. Inguimb., MS. 1775, fol. 5r.

[24] Peiresc to Théodore Godefroy, 8 August 1633, Paris, Bibliothèque de l'Institut, MS. Godefroy 493, fol. 358r.

[25] Carp., Bib. Inguimb., MS. 1775, fol. 5r: "De s'informer particulierement des officiers de la marine en ladit ville de Barcelonne, ou autres persones curieuses de vieulx livres, s'il se trouveroit un ou plusieurs libvres escriptes à la main, soit en parchemin ou en papier, ou aulcuns registres de ladit cour des consuls de mer, ou d'autres tribunaulx de justice, ou bien dans les Archives de l'Hostel de Ville de Barcellone. Dans lesquels registres, ou livres MSS fussent inserees lesdit loix ou coustumes de la mer."

[26] "Particulierement aux cinq premiers articles, and principalement au cinquiesme concernant l'approbation qu'on presuppose avoir esté faicte à Marseille. Et s'il s'en trouve ou lesdit articles soient inserez, il les fault collationner exactement, mot par mot et lettre par lettre, et marquer au marge de ladit coppie cy joincte toutes les diverses leçons et differances qui s'y recognoistront, soit aux chiffres & nombres, ou aux noms propres, ou au restant des paroles desdit articles quand mesmes il sembleroit qu'il y eust de l'incongruité, afin d'y pouvoir fonder telles conjectures qui y pourront escheoir." Carp., Bib. Inguimb., MS. 1775, fol. 5v.

[27] Carp., Bib. Inguimb., MS. 1775, fols. 5r–v; Carp., Bib. Inguimb., MS. 1792, fol. 578v.

[28] Carp., Bib. Inguimb., MS. 1775, fols. 5v.

[29] Peiresc seems first to have come into contact with him as the superior whose permission was required for Father Théophile Minuti's voyage to the Levant as Peiresc's agent in 1629. Peiresc's first surviving letter to Father François is a thank-you note for granting said permission, dated to 14 February 1629 (Carp., Bib. Inguimb., MS. 1876, fol. 375r). Jean François arrived in Barcelona at the end of April 1629 (Jean François to Peiresc, 8 May 1629, Carp., Bib. Inguimb., MS. 1816, fol. 243r).

[30] Whereas the other memo was not located in time or space, Carp., Bib. Inguimb., MS. 1816, fol. 229-31 is indexed as "SCHEDAE/ RIUIPOLLENSES/ & BARCINONAE/ par le P. Jean François Provincial des Minimes allant au Chappitre à Barcellone. 1629."

[31] Carp., Bib. Inguimb., MS. 1816, fol. 230r: "ou fussent attachez les vieux seaulx, prendre la description d'iceulx la plus exacte que faire se pourrà... Et si on les pourroit faire mouller et en prendre des empreintes au moins du visage ce la seroit bien curieux."

[32] Carp., Bib. Inguimb., MS. 1816, fol. 230r: "S'il y a des statües, ou peintures desdits Princes, sur les portes, aux vittres, dans les autels ou sur les reliquaires, calices, croix & autres utensiles de l'eglise on les pourroit aussy remarquer."

[33] Paris, B.N., MS. N.a.f. 5171, Peiresc to Guillemin, 1 June, 1609, fol. 708, published in *Lettres de Peiresc*, V, 231–233. At least some of this iconographic research project was completed, and survives (Carp., Bib. Inguimb., MS. 1784, fols. 119–131). The title page at fol. 119 reads "PORTRAITS DES PRINCES ET PRINCESSES DE LA MAISON D'ANIOU apportez d'Angers par le Prieur de Roumoules." These include a fine pencil sketch of Marie of Provence, sister of René of Anjou and wife of Charles VII, and beautiful miniature paintings of Louis II and his wife, Yolande of Aragon (Carp., Bib. Inguimb., MS. 1784, fols. 122r and 125v–126r). There is also the drawing of an unidentified female's tomb sculpture (fol. 124r).

[34] "... ne'quali non dubito che non si trovassero, sigili dove siamo rappresentate le lor figure, con gli habiti ò arme usate in que' secoli." Peiresc to Barberini, undated

[late 1625?], Vatican City, Biblioteca Apostolica Vaticana, MS. Barberini-Latina 6503, fol. 1r.

[35] Carp., Bib. Inguimb., MS. 1816, fol. 230v. Louis Aubery, one of Peiresc's helpers in the Barberini *famiglia*, explained to Peiresc that the Cardinal prevented him from leaving the legation in Madrid and going to Barcelona to do this research (Aubery to Peiresc, 17 October 1626, Paris, B.N., F.fr. 9542, fol. 218v).

[36] Carp., Bib. Inguimb., MS. 1816, fol. 231r: "Pour bien recognoistre si la maniere des portraicts qu'on trouverà là, aurà de la correspondance à la maniere antique du temps de ce prince, on a joinct à ce memoire une couple de petits monnoyes d'argent battüe en Provence de l'authorité dudit Roy Aldefons [*sic*] le Chaste, lors qu'il en possedoit la souveraineté." On the broader use of coins as proofs, see Federica Missere Fontana, *Testimoni parlanti. Le monete antiche a Roma tra Cinquecento e Seicento* (Roma: Edizioni Quasar, 2009).

[37] Carp., Bib. Inguimb., MS. 1816, fol. 231r: "& pour juger s'il y a du rapport des uns aux autres attendue que s'il ne s'y en trouve, c'est une marque infaillible que les portraicts ne seroit pas fidelles, attendu que ceux de la monoye du temps ne peuvent pas estre revocquez en doubte, pour la facon des habillements, ou couronnes, & de porter barbe ou non. Car pour la ressemblance du visage, la pettitesse des monoyes ne souffroit pas d'y pouvoir estre exactement observee par des ouvriers si grossiers que ceux de ce temps là."

[38] Carp., Bib. Inguimb., MS. 1816, fol. 231r: "a fin de comparer le portraict dudit Prince (qui y est representé rasé ayant une couronne fort simple et grossiere), avec les portraicts ou statües des tombeaux ou des frontispieces d'eglises, ou des autels, vitres, reliquaires, calices & autres vases de l'eglise et autres lieux, ou tels portraicts pourroient avoir esté conservez."

[39] Carp., Bib. Inguimb., MS. 1816, fol. 231r: "pour les tombeaux, epitaphes, armoires, statües ou portraicts desdit princes & princesses, faict sur les portes des eglises & chapelles, autels, victres, reliquaires, croix, calices & autres vases & utensiles de l'eglise. Et specialement, pour les chroniques MSS, anniversaires, chartres & documents anciens, et des seaulx du Roy Ildefons le Chate & de ses ayeulx & ayeulle."

[40] Carp., Bib. Inguimb., MS. 1816, fol. 231r. The Minim's father's researches—on the abbots of Ripoll from 888 (fols. 233–234r) or the epitaphs of Raymond Berenger (fol. 235r) and his donations to the monastery (fols. 236–237), including inscriptions and monograms (fol. 238)—were sent to Peiresc.

[41] Jean François to Peiresc, 16 May 1629, Carp., Bib. Inguimb., MS. 1816, fol. 245r.

[42] Carp., Bib. Inguimb., MS. 1881, fol. 70r, 71r.

[43] Carp., Bib. Inguimb., MS. 1881, fol. 71r.

[44] Carp., Bib. Inguimb., MS. 1775, fols. 9r–10r. "Extraits du Libvre du consulat de la mer, imprimé a Barcelone, l'an 1523, in 4.° par Dimas Bellestar et Jean de Gilioi, au feuillet 105 ou c.v. verso. Ils se trouvent pareillement quasi en mesmes termes en l'edition plus recente de l'an 1592 in fol.° chez Honostre Guari, au feuillet 102."

[45] But note that Philip I was King in 1102, that the future Louis VI was not in Acre in 1102, and that Acre was itself not captured from the Muslims until 1104.

[46] Carp., Bib. Inguimb., MS. 1775, fols. 9r–10

[47] Peiresc to Dupuy, 16 May 1627, *Lettres de Peiresc*, I, 230. For the earlier collaboration of the three men on medieval documentary history, see Miller "The Ancient Constitution and the Genealogist," 13.

[48] On the Assises, see Peter W. Edbury, *John of Ibelin and the Kingdom of Jerusalem* (Woodbridge and Rochester: Boydell Press, 1997); idem, "The Ibelin counts of Jaffa: A previously unknown passage from the 'Lignages d'Outremer'" in *Kingdoms of the Crusaders: From Jerusalem to Cyprus* (Aldershot: Ashgate, 1999), chp. VI, 604–610; and now *John of Ibelin. Le Livre des Assises*, ed. Peter W. Edbury (Leiden: Brill, 2003). The classic texts are M. Grandeclaude, "Classement sommaire des manuscrits des principaux livres des Assises de Jerusalem," *Revue historique de droit français et etranger*, ser. 4, 5 (1926) 459–462 and E.Brayer, P.Lemerle, and V.Laurent, "Le 'Vaticanus latinus 4789' histoire et alliances des Cantacuzenes aux xive–xve siecles," *Revue des études byzantines*, 9 (1951), 47–105.

[49] In April 1617 Peiresc wrote from Paris to a friend from his law school days in Padua, Lorenzo Pignoria: "Ho veduto mentione di un certo libro stampato in Cypro gia lungo tempo in foglio picolo intitolato le Assise di Gierusalem, tradotto dalla lengua Francese vecchia in volgare Italiana ove si contengono le leggi editti pragmatiche & altre ordinationi fatte in oriente da' prencipi Francesi. Et ho inteso che nella libraria di San Marco ce ne un essemplare MS^{to} in lengua Francese di que tempi, sarebbe cosa molto meritevole di trovare un essemplare di detta editione & farlo ristampare ò vero se si potesse haver copia dell'original Francese, lo facessimo stampare qui prout iacet nell'originale con una version appresso, come si fece gia del Villardoin." Peiresc to Pignoria, 12 April 1617, Carp., Bib. Inguimb., MS. 1875, fol. 338v. There was a Venetian copy of the Assises, and also an earlier printing (see Grandclaude, "Classement sommaire").

[50] Carp., Bib. Inguimb., MS. 1786, fols. 396v, 397v, 398r, 398v, 399r.

[51] Peiresc to Dupuy, 8 April 1627, *Lettres de Peiresc*, I, 196–197.

[52] Peiresc to Dupuy, 16 May 1627, *Lettres de Peiresc*, I, 221. He repeated this in his letter of 5 June 1627, *Lettres de Peiresc*, I, 265. Peiresc's own archive shows that these letters were actually written a month later.

[53] The cover letter to Danmartin included a request for a book, but the letter to Espannet referred to an enclosed list of books to buy, now missing, mentioning in passing that he expected these might be found "in the hands of Christian priests or other inhabitants of the Kingdom of Cyprus." Peiresc to Danmartin, 24 June 1627, Carp., Bib. Inguimb., MS. 1876, fol. 615r; Peiresc to Espannet, 24 June 1627, Carp., Bib. Inguimb., MS. 1876, fol. 615v.

[54] Peiresc to Dupuy, 17 July 1627, *Lettres de Peiresc*, I, 293. In a letter of 20 June 1627, Aleandro promised to look for a copy in the Vatican (Aleandro to Peiresc, Paris, B.N., MS. F.fr. 9541, f. 236r). News of Suares' discovery was conveyed in Aleandro's letter of 2 July 1627 (Paris, B.N., MS. F.fr. 9541, fol. 238r.)

[55] On the flyleaf of the letter from Suares to Peiresc of 27 August 1627, Peiresc wrote: "avec l'indice des chappitres des Assises de Jerusalem" (Paris, B.N., MS. F.fr. 9537, fol. 171v).

[56] Peiresc to Dupuy, 16 November 1627, *Lettres de Peiresc*, I, 420.

[57] Peiresc to Viguier, 28 November 1627, Carp. Bib. Inguimb., MS. 1876, fol. 615v.

[58] Peiresc to Danmartin, 25 November 1627, Carp., Bib. Inguimb., MS. 1873, fol. 122v.

[59] Paris, B.N., MS. N.a.f. 5169, fol. 29r, for 28 November 1627.

[60] To Dupuy, on 8 December 1627, Peiresc noted that there were three manuscripts sitting in quarantine in the bay of Marseille, and that he also expected to receive a copy of the 1535 Venice edition of the *Assises* within a few days. *Lettres de Peiresc*, I, 436. The copy was in his hand a day later (Peiresc to Dupuy, 9 December 1627, *Lettres de Peiresc*, I, 441–442).

[61] Paris, B.N., MS. N.a.f. 5169, fol. 29v, for 13 December 1627.

[62] Peiresc to Dupuy, 18–25 December 1627, *Lettres de Peiresc*, I, 444–450. The manuscript was published by Henri de Valois—dedicatee of Gassendi's *Vita Peireskii*—in 1638.

[63] Peiresc to Espannet, 13 December 1627, Carp., Bib. Inguimb., MS. 1873, fols. 122v–123r: "[D]es loix maritimes du Consulat de mer ou pour mieux dire des negotiantz, au long de la marine & des armementz de mer, encore que ce livre se soit imprimé soient en diverse langues, Catalane, Francoise, ou Italien...ne vous lassez point en la recherche du livre de LA HAULTE COURT ou des ASSISES & bonne usage du ROYAULME DE IERUSALEM. Et en celluy de la BASSE COURT, ou de la Cour du Vicomte de duc [sic] Bourgoine que se trouvent communement jointz ensemble et quand mesme vous rencontrerez de ceux qui furent traduictz en Italien et imprimez a Venize l'an 1535 soubz le tiltre de LALTA CORTE."

[64] Paris, B.N., MS. N.a.f. 5169, fol. 29v, 17 December 1627.

[65] Paris, B.N., MS. N.a.f. 5169, fol. 33r, 26 May 1628. The copy of the "Assises de Jerusalem" that Peiresc obtained from Cardinal Francesco Barberini in May 1628 was made from an early fifteenth-century copy of a version produced in Cyprus in 1369. On its first page Peiresc wrote, "Ce manuscrit est un des plus rares et des plus curieux de la bibliotheque vaticane, Monsig.ʳ le Cardinal Barberin me le fit transcrire non sans grand soin et peine" (Carp., Bib. Inguimb., MS. 1786, fol. 1r). We now know that the Roman copy was the sole exemplar of a second recension of the Assises and Peiresc's endeavor to obtain a copy brought it to France, where he had it copied for the Dupuy (now Paris, B.N., MS. Dupuy 652). It was the progenitor of six manuscript copies, as well as the first printed edition, edited by G. Thaumas de La Taumassière, *Coustumes de Beauvoisies, par Messire Philippes de Beaumanoir Bailly de Clermont en Beauvoisis. Assises et bons usages du royaume de Jerusalem, par Messire Jean d'Ibelin comte de Japhe et d'Ascalan, sire de Rames et de Baruth. Et autres anciennes coustumes le tout tiré des Manuscripts* (Bourges: Fr. Toubau, 1690).

[66] In 1631 Peiresc drew up a shopping list for Espannet (Carp., Bib. Inguimb., MS. 1769, fol. 242r–v).

[67] It is from a later redaction (1305 v. 1270); on this see Edbury, "The Ibelin Counts of Jaffa," 604–605; idem, *John of Ibelin. Le Livre des Assises*, 20; Marie-Adélaïde Nielen-Vandervoorde, "L'origine des croisés d'après les *Lignages d'Outremer*," *Orient et Occident du IXe au XVe siècle*, Georges Jehel, ed., intro. Robert-Henri Bautier, concl. Jean Richard (Paris: Éditions du temps, 2000), 95–104. Richard has elsewhere called attention to "l'abondance des noms de personnes et de lieux, notés dans une

langue très particulière" (in *Lignages d'Outremer*, ed. Marie-Adélaïde Nielen, (Paris: Académie des Inscriptions et Belles-Lettres, 2003), "Avant-Propos," 8.

[68] Peiresc to Dupuy, 18 December 1627, *Lettres de Peiresc*, I, 452.

[69] Peiresc to [De Loches], 14 December 1628, Carp. Bib., Inguimb., MS. 1876, fol. 374r. In Peiresc's register of outgoing correspondence this letter is listed as sent to a "P._____ Cappucin de Seyde" (Paris, B.N. MS. N.a.f. 5169, fol. 37v). We know that de Loches arrived there in 1626 but it was only F.A. de Thou's visit in 1629 that brought his name to Peiresc's attention.

[70] "Pour ce que memoire d'houme est desfaillant, car l'home faut que a mourir luy convient, pour ce convient a mettre en escript pour savoir les choses passées, car se escrire n'en fust nous ne savons rien les fais, ne les dis des anciens, qui sont trespasses grant tans a de ce siecle. Et pour ce avons vouleu faire cette remembrance de partie de la gent de sa mer, cest a savoir du Royaume de Jerusalem & de Chipre, d'Antioche et de Ermenie & de Triple pour savoir dont il sont estraict & venu & pour ce que li Roy ont estes & sont chef des autres nous commencerons premierent d'eaus ... Ci dit des Roys de Jerusalem." Carp., Bib. Inguimb., MS. 1786, fol. 403r (orthography is corrected in the edition of Rome, B.A.V., MS. Vaticana-Latina 4789 printed in *Lignages d' Outremer*, 85). Peiresc would have found this sentiment especially congenial; see Miller, *Peiresc's Europe*, chp. 5.

[71] A sample of this texture is found in an account of the heirs of Gui de Milli of Bessan (the modern Beit She'an): "The first Lord of Bessan was the brother of Lavene of Bessan, and married Betune and had a son Adam, who was Lord of Bessan, and maried a wife and had a son Gremont who was Lord of Bessan, and married Agnes the daughter of Hugh Lord of Giblet, and had four sons and threee daughters: Ades, Gautier and Amauri, and Philippe, Richet, Isabeau & Estefemie. Amauri and Philippe dying, Richent married Baudian of Ibelin, as was said. Isabeau married the Constable of Tabarie. Estefemie married Philippe le Rous and had Isabeau who was the mother of Emeri, Barlais. Ades married Helius the daughter of Henri the Buffalo" (Carp., Bib. Inguimb., MS. 1786, fols. 415v–416v). In later generations of this family we also find Porcellets (viz. Carp., Bib. Inguimb., MS. 1786, fols. 417r, 419r).

[72] "L'imprimeur au lecteur," *Le Consulat, contenant les Loix, Statuts, Coustumes touchant les Contracts, marchandises, & negociation Maritime* (Aix: David, 1635).

[73] Peiresc to Gaetano, 6 March 1637, Carp. MS. 1873, fol. 172v (postscript): "Saprei volontiere ancora se le ha mai passato per le mani alcun MSS.° del libro ord.ºⁱᵒ del Consulato di Mare, in lengua volgare Francese ò Catalana, ò Provenzale, che se ne caverebbe forzi qualche frutto, prencipalmente della sottoscrittione de prencipi et Republiche della Christianità che concorsero à farne l'approbation fra le quali quella di Pisa fu delli prime, che diedero il moto all'altre. Et se in Roma si trovarebbe alcuna memoria nelli registri publici del Campidoglio, ò d'altrove dove si facesse mentione delle leggi maritime antique & delli consoli stabiliti per esseguirle." A second, and final, letter from Peiresc to Gaetano, written only a few weeks before his death, shows Peiresc still hunting for sources, thanking him for the news "che nell'Archivio della Reformassioni di Firenze si conservano ancora gli stromenti & privileggi antiqui della Repub. di Pisa." Peiresc to Gaetano, 3 June 1637, Paris, B.N. MS. Naf. 5172, fol. 81r [= Carp. Bib. Inguimb., MS. 1873, fol. 177r]. For more on

Gaetano, see José Ruysschaert, "Constantino Gaetano, OSB, Chasseur de manuscrits. Contribution a l'histoire de de trois bibliotheques romaines de XVIIe siecle: L'*Anciana*, l'*Alessandrina*, et la *Chigi*" in *Mélanges Eugène Tisserant*, 7 vols. (Vatican City: Biblioteca Apostolica Vaticana, 1964), 7: 261–319; idem, "Trois notes pour une biographie du bénédictin Constantino Gaetano (1568–1650)," *Benedictina* 21 (1974) 215–223; and Dante Balboni, "L'Abate Constantino Gaetani (1568–1650), editore delle opere di S. Pier Damiam (1606–40)," in *Ascetica cristiana e ascetica giansenista e quietista nelle regioni d'influenza avellanita: Atti del I convegno del Centro di Studi Avellanti. Fonte Avellana* 19 (Fonte Avellana: Il Centro, 1978),110–125.

[74] Peiresc to Gaetano, 6 March 1637, Carp. MS. 1873, fol. 172v: "i primi da Christiani a dar intaccio all'imperio maritimo che da tanti anni prima possederano li Sarraceni & di acquistar una buona parte."

[75] This passage, in which he refers to "vir sane eruditissimus clarissimusque Claudius Nicolaus Fabricius Peyrescius Gallus, de litteris deque litteratis bene merentissimus" is in notes on Pandolpho's life of Pope Gelasius II, printed in Ludovico Muratori, *Rerum Italicarum scriptores* (vol. 3, part I, 402ff. Milano: A. Forni, 1975) and quoted in Jean-Marie Pardessus, *Collection de lois maritimes antérieures au XVIIIe siècle*, 6 vols. (Paris: Imprimé royale, 1828–1845), 12. Pardessus shows that Gaetano's patriotic history was false (14–15).

[76] Capmany was the first person to question the authenticity of this document in his *Memorias historicas sobre la marina, &c., de Barcelona* according to Pardessus, *Collection de lois maritimes antérieures*, 5. Pardessus' demolition of the ratification dates by source critique is most thorough (7–11).

[77] The *Lignages d'Outremer* would only be published in the later nineteenth century amid French enthusiasm for Outremer. Might Du Cange have known anything about Peiresc's researches? This is likely, but it is a question no one has asked. The new edition of the *Lignages d'Outremer* does not even indicate Peiresc's ownership of the paradigmatic manuscript.

[78] Steven Runciman, *The Families of Outremer. The Feudal Nobility of the Crusader Kingdom of Jerusalem, 1099–1291. The Creighton Lecture in History 1959* (London: Athlone Press, 1960).

[79] Jean Richard, *Le Comté de Tripoli sous la dynastie toulousaine (1102–1187)* (Paris: Société nouvelle librairie orientaliste Paul Geuthner, 1945), 90. I follow Peiresc's spelling, though the current convention is "Porcelet." Richard followed the hint dropped by Fernand Benoit, "Les Porcellets de Syrie," *Congrès de Marseille 4–7 April 1929. Comptes Rendus et Mémoires* (Marseille: Au siège de l'Institut, 1930), 33–37.

[80] Carp., Bib. Inguimb., MS. 1844, 1845. The scale of this dwarfs the scope of Peiresc's study of other families, even substantial studies, such as that devoted to the Villeneuve family of Les Arcs and later Vence, see Carp., Bib. Inguimb., MS. 1848, fols. 109–209; MS. 1881, fols. 304r–330v.

[81] For example, Carp., Bib. Inguimb., MS. 1844, fol. 11r, fol. 21r; Carp., Bib. Inguimb., MS. 1845, fols. 43–47.

[82] Many of the same documents are now being mined by contemporary scholars, and for many of the same reasons. See Damien Carraz, "Les ordres militaires et la

ville (XIIe–XIIIe siècles). L'exemple des commanderies urbaines de la basse vallée du Rhône," *Annales du Midi*, 239 (2002), 275–292; Daniel Le Blévec, Alain Venturini, "Cartulaire des ordres militaires, XIIe–XIIIe siècles (Provence occidentale—basse vallée du Rhone)," *Les cartulaires. Actes de la table ronde organisée par l'Ecole national des chartes et le GDR 121 du CNRS*, Olivier Guyotjeannin, Laurent Morelle, and Michel Parise, eds. (Paris: École des Chartes, 1993), 451–466; Daniel Le Blévec, Alain Venturini, *Cartulaire du prieuré de Saint-Gilles de l'Hôpital de Saint-Jean de Jérusalem (1129–1210)* (Paris-Turnhout: Brepols, 1997); Dominic Selwood, *Knights of the Cloister. Templars and Hospitallers in Central-Southern Occitania (1100–1300)* (Woodbridge: Boydell Press, 1999); and on this, Damien Carraz, "Templiers et hospitaliers en France méridionale (XIIe–XIIIe siècles). A propos d'un ouvrage récent," *Provence Historique* 50 (2000), 207–237. For the documentary base, see Archives Départmentales des Bouches-du-Rhone, *Répertoire de la Série H: 56 H: Grand Prieuré de Saint-Gilles des Hospitaliers de Saint-Jean de Jérusalem*, établi par Édouard Baratier and Madeleine Villard (Marseille: Archives Départementales, 1966); *Cartulaire general de l'ordre des Hospitaliers de Saint-Jean de Jerusalem (1100–1310) vol. II (1201–60)*, J. Delaville Le Roulx, ed. (Paris: E.Leroux, 1897).

[83] Dominic Selwood notes that the military orders are generally ignored by those who write about monasticism, whereas those who write about the orders in the Crusades rarely consider their European manifestation; see *Knights of the Cloister*, 2. Carp., Bib. Inguimb., MS. 1816, fol. 598r bears the penciled heading "Ex Cartologio Templariorum St Egidii." On this cartulary see Damien Carraz, "Le cartulaire du temple de Saint-Gilles, outil de Gestion et instrument de pouvoir" *Les Cartulaires méridionaux*, Daniel le Blévec, ed. (Paris: Droz, 2006) 145–162.

[84] Jean Richard, "Le comté de Tripoli dans les chartes du fonds des Porcellet," *Bibliothèque de l'École des chartes*, 130 (1972), 339–382, at 366. I thank Brigitte Bedos-Rezak for bringing this to my attention. Here, too, Benoit's 1929 conference paper proved seminal (see above, note 79). Martin Aurell has linked the rise in surviving documentation on the Porcellet family with the installation of the military orders in the Camargue and Rhone regions (*Actes de la famille Porcelet d'Arles (972–1320). Collection de documents inédits sur l'histoire de France. Section d'histoire et philologie des civilisations médiévales. Série in -8°-vol. 27. Paris: C[omité des] T[ravaux] H[istoriques et] S[cientifiques]*, 2001), xiii.

[85] Carp., Bib. Inguimb., MS. 1844, fol. 21v.

[86] Aurell identifies the themes of these documents with the "multiples facettes de la société, les pouvoirs, la religion ou l'économie en Méditerranée occidentale." *Actes de la famille Porcelet d'Arles (972–1320)*, xii. Aurell notes the existence of Peiresc's two volumes in Carpentras but seems not to have viewed them. Moreover, he assimilates Peiresc's purpose to Pierre d'Hozier's interest in verifying proofs of nobility (xix–xx). Peiresc is not mentioned at all in his dissertation, *Une famille de la noblesse provençale au Moyen Age, les Porcelet* (Avignon: Aubanel, 1986). A similar project might be W.H. Rudt de Collenberg's study of "Les 'Raynouard', seigneurs de Nephin et de Maraclé en Terre sainte, et leur parenté en Languedoc," in de Collenberg, *Familles de l'Orient latin XIIe–XIVe siecles* (Ashgate: Farnham, 1983), chp. II.

[87] One set of notes (Carp., Bib. Inguimb., MS. 1844, fols. 292r–95), unlike many of the others, was created as a digest and was arranged chronologically, rather than by a given document's foliation. We also find subsections devoted to specific locations (viz. Fos and Maillane: Carp., Bib. Inguimb., MS. 1844, fol. 293v; Provence: Carp., Bib. Inguimb., MS. 1844, fol. 295r–v). A fair copy of this is found in Avignon, Bibliothèque Municipale, MS. 4880, fols. 56–77.

[88] Carp., Bib. Inguimb., MS. 1844, fols. 298, fol. 342r. This was found in "Registro Regis Caroli I signato 1271, lra B. fol. 87." A first passage is marked "In registro Regis Caroli Primi signato 1276 lra A fol. 114" and others follow for the years 1276, 1269, 1271, 1275, 1270, 1277, 1274, each given with its precise reference to volume and page (Carp., Bib. Inguimb., MS. 1844, fols. 342–346).

[89] From Genoa, he received from one Pietro Paolo Mellegani a list of the Genoese Porcellets collated by year from 1136 to 1590 (Carp., Bib. Inguimb., MS. 1844, fols. 299–300; 327r). Other information about the Genoese Porci, Porcelli and Striglia Porci came from Naples (Carp., Bib. Inguimb., MS. 1845, fols. 122–125). Information on the Spanish branch of the family came from Juan de Mariana in Spain, in letters of December 1605 and June 1606 (Carp., Bib. Inguimb., MS. 1844, fols. 335, 337). Another letter, from Pietro Vincenti, archivist in Naples, to the Bishop of Toul, dates from March 1606 (Carp., Bib. Inguimb., MS., fol. 339).

[90] Aurell has hinted (*Porcellet*, xv) at the usefulness of the collection of Porcellet documents copied out in Avignon for reconstituting materials lost in the German firing of the Neapolitan Archive in 1943, but as he did not examine the Peiresc materials the utility of his archive for making good those losses cannot be resolved yet. Damien Carraz, by contrast, has collated copies of Porcellet material in Carpentras MS 1845 with actes in the Cartulaire du Temple de Saint-Gilles now in the Bibliothèque municipale d'Arles ("Le Cartulaire du Temple de Saint-Gilles," *Les cartulaires*, 146n6.)

[91] "& altri dell famiglia Porcelletta vennero in regno con Carlo Con. di Provenza che fa re di Napoli, dopo la vittoria contro Manfredi & Corradino" (Carp., Bib. Inguimb., MS. 1844, fol. 298r). Peiresc's archive contains a copy of the excerpt made in that archive of the concession to Guillaume Porcellet of the castles of Calatamauri and Calatafimi on 18 July 1271 (found in "Registro Regis Caroli I Sig.to 1271, lra B. fol. 87"), Carp., Bib. Inguimb., MS. 1844, fol. 342r.

[92] Carp., Bib. Inguimb., MS. 1844, fol. 398v.

[93] "Indices sive potius quaaedam summae monumentorum familiae Porcelletae regio in Archivio Siciliae et Neapolis sistentium. Quae summae exinde facti substantia non mutata collectae sunt atque descriptae A. D. Petro Vincentio," Carp., Bib. Inguimb., MS. 1844, fols. 303–324. Vincenti's preface is dated 9 March 1603 (305r).

[94] Carp., Bib. Inguimb., MS 1844, fol. 306r.

[95] The excerpts from Ammirato begin on fol. 318r. Peiresc's interest in Ammirato's *History* continued for some time; he includes it in a list of books on the history of Italian families in a letter to a French gentleman traveling in Rome in 1631 (Peiresc to Du Buisson, 24 August 1631, Carp., Bib. Inguimb., MS. 1872, fol. 536r).

[96] Carp., Bib. Inguimb., MS. 1844, fols. 325r–331v.

[97] "Catalogus continens nomina aliquot virorum illustrium qui Andegavensi sub regali domo Neapolim, urbem amenissimam et famosam, gubernarunt. Ad Praestantissimum Virum Jo'em Porcelletam de Maillana. A D.P. Vincentio," fol. 331v–332r. A copy of this with the name "Bertrandus Porcelletus, miles...1316" carefully underlined (along with those of several others) is found at 394r.

[98] Mariana to Jean de Porcellet, Bishop of Toul, 1 June 1606 (fol. 305v) and 23 October 1605 (fol. 337); Vincenti to Jean de Porcellet, 27 March 1606 (fol. 339); Luc[?] Antonio Porcelli to Bishop of Toul, 7 November 1607 (fol. 339v). Note that these letters conclude a separate but continously paginated group of documents that began with the excerpts from the historians of Aragon, viz. 325r–341r [I–XVII]. This suggests that an entire dossier of original material was transferred to Peiresc at some subsequent point.

[99] Thus, a first passage is marked "In registro Regis Caroli Primi signato 1276 lra A fol. 114" and others follow for the years 1276, 1269, 1271, 1275, 1270, 1277, 1274, each given with its precise reference to volume and page. A "Reynaldo Porcelleto" is the first mentioned; Carp., Bib. Inguimb., MS. 1844, fols. 342–346.

[100] Carp., Bib. Inguimb., MS 1844, fols. 347–352

[101] Carp., Bib. Inguimb., MS. 1844, fols. 353–361.

[102] Carp., Bib. Inguimb., MS. 1844, fols. 362–370.

[103] Carp., Bib. Inguimb., MS. 1844, fols. 371–377.

[104] Carp., Bib. Inguimb., MS. 1844, fol. 378–389.

[105] Carp., Bib. Inguimb., MS. 1845, fol. 204. We know, for instance, that attestations dated to 21 April 1607 and 5 December 1607 give the names of Jo. Battista de Juliis, Fabricius Sergius, and Octavius Athansius, omitting any reference to Vincenti) and that de Juliis had then the charge of Keeper of the Archive. Another undated attestation lists "Fabrice Sergius, greffier ordinaire de la Chambre royale et actuaire de magnifique personne Jean-Baptiste de Juliis, gard dudict archive royal," suggesting that Juliis held the position of Archivist *c.* 1606 but was replaced by Vincenti, while Sergius remained in place (Carp., Bib. Inguimb., MS. 1844, fol. 392v).

[106] "Le soubscrit notaire apostolique et imperial, demeurant a Nancy, atteste qu'il ha collationné les tiltres cy devant comprins en cinquante-trois feuillets, sur des copies tirées des registres originaulx qui se conservaent en l'archive royal de la grande cour royale de Sicile, par Fabrice Sergius, greffier ordinaire de la Chambre royale et actuaire de magnifique personne Jean-Baptiste de Juliis, gard dudict archive royal . . . avec la legalité y rapportée munie en seel royal, et que les present copies extraicts desdits autres copies se concordent de mot a mot." Carp., Bib. Inguimb., MS. 1844, fol. 392v.

[107] Carp., Bib. Inguimb., MS 1845, fol. 15ter r.

[108] Carp., Bib. Inguimb., MS 1845, fols. 212–216r.

[109] Lists are Carp., Bib. Inguimb., MS. 1845, fols. 216r–221r. Between the narrative and the lists the author added a fatherly injunction, in French and in first person: "Mon fils, j'ay adjousté les maisons desquelles vous estes descendu en ligne directe par voz meres & Ayeulz affin qu'honnoriez & serviez tous ceux qui en sont descendus, & a qui vous avez l'honneur d'appartenir" (fol. 219v–220r).

[110] Carp., Bib. Inguimb., MS. 1845, fols. 221–230r. Peiresc also retained the excerpts from the "livre noyr" (253v and 253bis r).

[111] Carp., Bib. Inguimb., MS. 1845, fols. 126bis–131r.

[112] Carp., Bib. Inguimb., MS. 1844, fols. 413–420: *Ioannis S.R.I. Baronis Porceleti Maillanei S.D.N. Cubicularii Secreti. Oratio De sanctissimi nominis IESV dignitate. Habita in sacello pontificio die circumcisioni Dominicae sacra anno domini MDCVI* (Rome: Aloisium Zannettum, 1606), in 4-o, 13p +[2].

[113] Carp., Bib. Inguimb., MS. 1844, fols. 404r–412r: *Panegyricus Ioanni Porceleto Maillanae in petitione I.V. Licentiae, idibus Aug. 1604. In Auditorio I. V. Pontimussa-no . . . Autore Nicolao Guineto J.V. In Academia Pontimussana Professore ordinario* (Pontimussi: F. Dubois et viduam N. Claudet, 1605), in 4-o, 27 pp.

[114] The "Elenchus monimentorum, & autorum ex quibus Porceleti Stemmatis Claritas est collecta" includes public acts from the city of Arles going back to the twelfth century, from the Neapolitan archives from 1270, 1271, 1282 etc., from the Acts of the City of Arles, as well as from the histories of Ammirato, Mariana, Morales, and Fazellus. *Panegyricus*, sig. D2v-D3r, paginated as Carp., Bib. Inguimb., MS. 1844, fols. 411v–412r.

[115] "Reg. Archiv. Aquens. Ex Lotharing./ Achiv Arelat. [from the archdeacon] Claretus, du Sr de Maillane d'Arles, Massil[ia], Sylvacane, Digne, du Sr. de Maillane d'Arles pour Dragonet." Carp., Bib. Inguimb., MS. 1844, fol. 421r.

[116] "Extraict de l'inventaire des tiltres inventorisez a Aix en Provence l'an 1301. reposant au thresor de St. A[ltesse] en la layette de Provence a Nancy." Carp., Bib. Inguimb., MS. 1844, fol. 421ter–425v.

[117] "[A]ux estats & quaternes des maisons des Roys de Naples & comptes de Provence, qui sont gardes en la dicte chambre des comptes, quels estats ceux de la maison des Pourcellets [sic] y ont eu et particulierement du temps du Roy Rene[,] du Roy Louis, car du temps de Charles 1.2 & Robert & Jeanne, il s'en treuve des tesmoignage de chambellans, conseillers, gouverneurs des enfents de Roy, d'escuriers d'escurierie, gouverneurs de la ville de Naples, du Duche d'Adelfe de la province d'Abruce." Carp., Bib. Inguimb., MS. 1844, fol. 425v.

[118] Carp., Bib. Inguimb., MS. 1845, fols. 23–25.

[119] Carp., Bib. Inguimb., MS. 1845, fols. 43, 47.

[120] Carp., Bib. Inguimb., MS. 1845, fols. 44–46.

[121] Carp., Bib. Inguimb., MS. 1845, fols. 13–14.

[122] Jean de Maillane, Bishop of Toul, to Peiresc, 16 June 1614, Carp., Bib. Inguimb., MS. 1845, fol. 231r. "Secondement vous portra un abrege de la cognoissance que nous avions de notre maison, ou je n'adiouste rien sinon que j'ay veu les denombre-ment des fiefs des Baronies de Calatafimi et Calatamauri possedeés par Guilaume Pourcelet qui se trouve viceroye de Sicile par un tiltre que j'ai recouvera depuis le deces de feu mon pere. Pour tiltres anciens je vous envoye la liste de ceux de mon Abbaye de S. Mansuit, vous aures la copie de ceux que vous me marqueres. Mais hors de cete abbaye je n'ay rien que fort recent, et hors de votre propos, car le plus ancien de mes aultres tiltres n'est que depuis quatre cent ans. Voila un bref le raport de tout ce que je vous puis dire pour notre entretien, et pour notre devoir et contantement."

[123] See above, Carp. Bib. Inguimb., MS. 1845, fols. 212–230.

[124] Carp., Bib. Inguimb., MS. 1845, fol. 247. For discussion of some of the cartularies from which these were excerpted, see Carraz, "Le cartulaire du temple de Saint-Gilles, outil de Gestion et instrument de pouvoir," 145–146.

[125] Carp., Bib. Inguimb., MS. 1845, fol. 247v.

[126] Jules Lieure, *Jacques Callot. Catalogue raisonné de l'oeuvre gravé*, 2 vols. (San Francisco: Alan Wofsy Fine Arts, 1989 [rpt]) I, 26. The copy in the Cabinet des Estampes (Res.) of the Bibliothèque Nationale in Paris is believed unique.

[127] Mention of Peiresc's copy of Callot's print was omitted from the late-nineteenth and early twentieth-century printed catalogue of Peiresc's papers at Carpentras and as a result seems to have escaped the attention of researchers (Carp., Bib. Inguimb., MS. 1844, fol. 420ter).

[128] Recent models of movement-as-cultural history are Bernard Bailyn, *Voyagers to the West* (New York: Knopf, 1986) and Michael McCormick, *The Origins of the European Economy 400–900: Communications and Commerce* (Cambridge: Cambridge University Press, 2000).

[129] The Callot *texts* resemble the digest in Peiresc's archive discussed above at n. 87 (Carp., Bib. Inguimb., MS. 1845, fols. 2–11).

[130] For a detailed description of "description," see Louis Marin, "Mimésis et Description. Ou de la curiosité à la méthode de l'âge de Montaigne à celui de Descartes," *Documentary*, 23–47; Miller, "Description Terminable and Interminable: Looking at the Past, Nature and Peoples in Peiresc's Archive," 355–397.

[131] Peiresc drew up a list of the Provençal archives he—and it was most likely he—explored, Carp., Bib. Inguimb., MS. 1844, fol. 421r.

[132] Peiresc's long autograph excerpt from Digne (in an early Latin hand) referring to Guillelmus Porcellet for the year 1324 is followed, condensed, by Callot (Carp., Bib. Inguimb., MS. 1844, fol. 454r).

[133] Daniel Ternois, *Jacques Callot. Catalogue complet de son oeuvre dessiné* (Paris: F. de Nobele, 1962), 20, 44. Callot's "Le Miracle de Saint Mansuy," executed at the end of his Florentine stay c. 1616, depicts the first bishop of Toul, who converted the Christians, in the guise of the current one (97).

[134] See Oliver Poncet, "Des Chartes pour un royaume. Les Prétensions de la famille de la Trémoille sur le royaume de Naples au XVIIIe siècle," *Annuaire-Bulletin de la Société de l'histoire de France* (2007), 145–172. More broadly, *Les 'La Trémoille' à Thouars—Huit siècles d'archives*, Frédérique Chauvenet, ed. (Thouars: Association Thouars Marguerite d'Écosse, 2006). The La Trémoille family is discussed during the disastrous dinner at the Verdurin's in which Swann is tweaked by M. de Forcheville (*Swann's Way*, I, 268–271).

IV

Peiresc's Medieval Mediterranean in the History of Historiography

⚜

AT SOME POINT, MOST LIKELY (but not definitely) after his return to Provence in 1623, Peiresc set out, whether on commission or on his own, to design a seal for the nobility of Provence. The basic historical reality to be accommodated visually was the union of France with Provence, but the quarter for Provence was to include the cross of Jerusalem. In a marginal addition to this note, Peiresc supplied the explicit historical explanation: "The arms of Jerusalem are mixed there because our Counts had borne them united with theirs for three hundred years without ever giving them up."[1]

Peiresc's awareness of the Crusasders' footprints at either end of the Mediterranean is registered in his deeply archival sensibility. If we compare his approach with that of contemporary editions of classics like Joinville and new collections of Crusade narratives such as Bongars's *Gesta dei per Francos* (1611), what we find is that his eye is turned away from narrative and toward the sources of these narratives. This is especially clear when we see him in action reading Bongars's collection for its usefulness in corroborating archival evidence.[2] By collecting and publishing Crusade narratives Bongars made a recognizable and much appreciated contribution to scholarship. What Peiresc was doing, by contrast, strip mining whole archives for scraps of information about Crusaders and their families—which he reconstituted in his own vision as his own archive—many of which told of obscure figures doing ordinary deeds like buying and selling, was extremely unusual. Indeed, as late as 1930 a scholar could signal the need to study the role of Provençaux in the Crusades.[3] Of course, Peiresc also found the Crusades far from the archives: on buildings in Paris,[4] in books,[5] on artifacts,[6] in coin collections,[7] and in literary texts.[8] Each of these "finds" in turn suggested to him a whole story onto which opened only the smallest window. This, too, went well beyond what most anyone else imagined "history" then to mean.[9]

Peiresc understood full well that his kind of historical scholarship required some explanation. Contrasting, for the benefit of Cardinal Francesco Barberini, Nostradamus's unreliable history of Provence with his own project, Peiresc emphasized both the importance of its archival basis and that this was history, not some *Hilfswissenschaft*. In the archive "one could learn the history of those times much more securely than all this that is said and written by badly informed people who have introduced a thousand lies and blunders, unworthy of memory. On the contrary, true history is buried and the memory of many things important and worthy of faith is wiped out. And it will be possible, without much difficulty, to pass it on to posterity from there."[10]

Peiresc may have come to the Crusades by following individual Provencaux as they moved across the Mediterranean, but it was the larger, Mediterranean-wide phenomenon that seems to have fired his imagination. It led him to rethink the history of key aspects of his own work: the history of French institutions, and the practice of history itself.

For Peiresc saw his archival research on the Crusades having an immediate impact on the history of the Parlement in France. In a series of excerpta he traced its role and qualities from the thirteenth century onward. What is interesting is the frequency with which he locates significant evidence for its development in a Crusading context, whether in Outremer or back in France, but occasioned by the needs of supporting Outremer. For example, from a manuscript describing the life of Louis VII that he found in St Denis he extracted material "De adventu regis Franciae in Hierusalem."[11] Ostensibly about King Baldwin's calling of a council in Jerusalem, it offers an overview of the legal structure in the East. "All the lands then held by the Christians in the transmarine parts," it began, were divided into four principal baronies: the King of Jerusalem, Count of Tripoly, Prince of Antioch, and Count of Rohes (Edessa), with the former the chief baron.[12] Like some modern scholars, Peiresc conceived of the power arrangements in the Kingdom of Jerusalem in terms of those current in twelfth-century France.[13] Looking at the Kingdom of Jerusalem from the vantage point of a seventeenth-century parlementaire just might have sharpened the contrast between present and past notions of the consultative and representative powers of the Parlement.[14] And so, when the Emperor and King of France called another Parlement, the text defines this as "where the Great Barons came together with the Minor ones as they did before."[15]

Similarly, for the year 1146, when King Louis decided to go off and fight the Turks, where a chronicler had written, "in that same year at the Castle of Vezelay, he brought together the great Parlement, where Archbishops, Bishops, Abbots and the greater part of the Barons of France gathered together," Peiresc tersely summarizes: "MAGNUM PARLAMENTUM/ VEZELIACI CASTRO."[16] Alongside the listing for the year 1149, Peiresc wrote in the margin "ORIENTES IV BARONIAE" and named them. In that year, the chronicler tells us that the German Emperor (Conrad), Louis VII King of France, the King of Jerusalem, the Patriarch "and the other Barons" ("et alii Barones") were gathered in Jerusalem "for that Parlement" ("ad illud Parlamentum"). An earlier annotator wrote in one margin "Parlement for the great assemblies" ("Parlement pour grandes assemblees"); in the other, Peiresc noted "Jerusalem Parlement" ("PARLAMENTUM HIEROSOLYMIT-ANUM".)[17]

After the return of the armies of the Emperor and French King a "Parlamentum" was held where "the great with the lesser Barons" ("magni Barones cum minoribus") gathered. The entry ended "solutum fut parlamentum." In the margin, Peiresc explained: "PARLAMENT where the great Barons gathered with the Lesser, SOLUTUM."[18] Back from the East, and facing the insurgency of the Duke of Normandy in 1153, the latter was summoned to, in Peiresc's words, the "Court of the French Kings" and the "Commission of the King's Palace."[19]

In 1179, again upon returning from the East, the seventy-year-old king called a general council for Paris. In the margin Peiresc wrote, "General Council of the Barons and the Bishops" ("GENERALE CONSILIUM/ EP[IS-COP]ORM BARONUM.")[20] In 1185 and 1186 there are other mentions of convoking the "consilio," the "Iudicium curiae regis," and the "consilium episcoporum ac principum maiores." In 1186 Philip II ("Augustus") convoked the "Council of the Barons and Bishops of the Land" ("CONSILIUM EPISCO-PORUM ET BARONUM TERRAE") to raise over the course of two years the tenth tax "vulgarly called the 'Saladine'."[21] Other councils were called in 1190 and 1205.[22] In 1224 Louis VIII called a "PARLAMENTUM GENER-ALE" to deal with consequences of the Albigensian Crusade—yet another Crusade.[23] And in the penultimate entry, for the year 1268, a PARLAMEN-TUM is called by Louis IX to go on Crusade.[24]

From Peiresc's choice of excerpts, and from Peiresc's annotation of these excerpts, we see him linking Crusading and the calling of an assembly of the Barons, which, by the second half of the thirteenth century, was typically termed a "Parlement."

Finally, in his most worked-out attempt to write the history of Parlement, Peiresc put Outremer at the precise heart of the story. "It was under King St Louis," he writes, "around the year 1254, after he had returned from his first voyage to Outremer, that he resolved by holy inspiration to be more assiduous than before in rendering justice to his subjects...and to this effect, upon his arrival at Paris convoked a great assembly of many Prelates and Barons and noble Clerics of all estates and men of his Council for advising on the making of justice"[25] (Figure 4.1). In a struck-through first version, Peiresc explained that, "He began to establish at a certain time in each year in which he went to expedite justice, which was called PARLEMENT."[26]

With this terminological question resolved, the bulk of the essay is devoted to an earlier period in which France was dominated by a variety of consultative institutions all of which could lay claim to a notion of "parlement" though they were called by different names. In effect, the drama of the essay is to look at "old" France, from Clovis, Childebert, and Clothaire to Louis IX and Philip the Fair.[27] What Peiresc discerned was nothing less than a parlementary

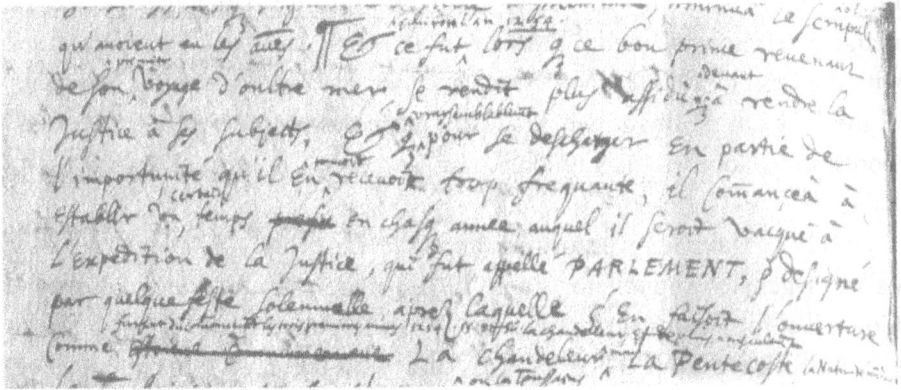

FIGURE 4.1 La Vraye Origine des Parlements, Conseils & aultres Cours souveraines du Royaulme de France. Carpentras, Bibliothèque Inguimbertine, MS. 1864, fol. 310v. Bibliothèque Inguimbertine, Archives et Musées de Carpentras.

society. There were the "parlements generaux du Royaume," the parlement around the person of the king and council, the parlements of Palais royal & courts, the parlements of the great provinces, the great parlements of each county or diocese, the little parlements of every vicounty or "century," and the parlements of the free townsmen, called "Mallobergii."[28]

Peiresc then turns to the systematic discussion of these different types of parlements and then to their transformation into the existing structure of French government.[29] What we do not find, however, is any reference at all to the government of Outremer, nor the nuanced sensitivity to the social reality of the parlements in Outremer that we see him attentive to in his underlinings and *adversaria*. Instead, we see Peiresc teasing out and reassembling the extensive tissue of parlements, *of various sorts*, that existed in France and that had by his own day been reduced to the law courts of Paris, Normandy, and Provence, to the latter of which, of course, he belonged.

The "Barons," when they make their appearance, are only five in number— the Dukes of Burgundy and Normandy, and the Counts of Toulouse, Flanders, and Champagne—and their category no longer admits of lesser and greater.[30] And yet, Peiresc does note that Louis VII sought to counterbalance their might with that of the peers ("Pairs") and prelates. And it was at this juncture in time that the name "Parlement" was associated with "meeting of the group."[31]

Peiresc's repeated reference to the role of the Barons is not an accident, and explaining its presence here shows us how, beginning with interest in the Crusades, itself drawn out of his attention to mobility in the Provençal Mediterranean, Peiresc came to one of the central debating points of his age:

the historical role of the Commons, or Third Estate. Discussion of the Barons was a central theme in the history of Parliament developed in the 1620s—likely when the essay was written—by his English correspondents, Sir Henry Spelman and John Selden. Richard Tuck argues that in the first edition of *Titles of Honour* (1614) Selden noted that originally the Parliament was composed of the greater, alongside the lesser, barons. Later, he observed, the category of "lesser" barons became that of "freeholders" and then, later still, the "Commons." Initially, then, Parliament in England was unicameral, as it still was in Scotland in Selden's day. It is in this note on "Barons" that Selden declines to comment on the French parlements.[32] This argument then became explicit in the second edition of *Titles of Honour*, which, although finally published in 1631, had been largely completed at the end of 1621, when publication was stayed.

There is no discussion of any of this in the Peiresc–Selden correspondence. Nor do we find explicit mention of it in the surviving letters of Peiresc to Spelman. (Of course this does not mean that they did not discuss this fact, only that we cannot prove that they discussed it.) We do know that Peiresc received a sample of Spelman's "Glossaire Archaeologique" before April 1619, and it may have contained some information about the barons.[33] And Peiresc did ask him for help distinguishing between "PAIRS du Royaulme," "PAIRS du païs" and "PAIRS du fief ou de la Cour."[34] In fact, Spelman's discussion of the "barons" was extensive and through etymological argument demonstrated unequivocally that historically "baron" had connoted common folk ("*Baro* pro *homine* simpliciter"), vassal or tenant and knight, though "today most notably" referred to "magnate."[35] And though now, Spelman continues, the custom had come to link the "*maiores Barones*" with the "Lords of Parliament" and it was common to say that "omnes totius Angliae *Barones* tam *minores* quam *maiores* locum aliquando in summis illis Comitiis obtinuisse," he thought it physically impossible for approximately 30,000 people ever to have convened.[36] The term itself, he thought, came to England from France with the Norman Conquest (he provided etymologies to support this claim.)[37] "Barones minores" he explicitly defined as lords of manors whose judiciary authority did not extend to matters of life and death.[38] And, finally, Spelman treated the Barons as part of the class of Peers and discussed this identity in the concluding part of the essay.[39] In the complete *Archaeologus*, published posthumously in 1687, there is a short entry devoted to "Pares" in which Spelman explicitly writes that the category of peer included "Rege, Comite & Barone (sive majore, sive minori)," suggesting the point of contact between Peiresc and the English scholars.[40]

So, Peiresc may have been reading his documents with an eye made sensitive by the work of his English friends, or he may have recognized the importance of this distinction on his own, and for his own reasons.

Why might Peiresc not have made an argument about the importance of the distinction between the "greater" and the "lesser" barons in his essay on the "origin of parlement" in France? Which is another way of asking why he dwelt so comprehensively there on the institutional history and not its social import. France, Peiresc argued, was a polity shaped by its parlements at every level. That this had changed beyond recognition could not itself change the past. In Selden's England, by contrast, where parliamentarianism had triumphed, by the 1620s the issue had shifted to the respective roles of Lords and Commons in the future, with all that followed from it. And in this context, the importance of the old distinction between "greater" and "lesser" barons loomed large.

Unlike his English friends, Peiresc came to this analysis of Parlement through the kind of historical work on the Crusades that no one else was doing. Another powerful outcome of his Crusades research was recognizing the importance of cross-cultural comparison. It was not enough to study Western Crusade texts, as Bongars proposed. Peiresc believed that one had also to read the Arab writers on the Crusades. "With what ardency ("Et quam ardenter")," Gassendi writes, "did he seek to get a translation and edition of those Arabic books which the most excellent Golius recently brought with him out of the East, containing a history of the expeditions and wars of our kings in Syria? For he thought it possible that writers of that nation might relate many things differently than ours, which would be worthwhile to know. So that, at the least, from comparing them together a more probable narration might be framed."[41]

And, moreover, comparative history could not be done from self-conscious narratives alone. Gassendi continued, turning now to the kind of archival research we have been analyzing.

> For he [Peiresc] was likewise of the opinion that many things omitted by our historians might be supplemented from those of that region, the various councils of the time, the charters, letters, seals, coats of arms, inscriptions, coins and other things of that sort. Now, he was extremely curious ("impense curiosus") about such things as these above all others, because he said they were incorrupted witnesses of antiquity, & that such things might be learned from them, which a man should seek in vain among all Historians extant.[42]

This is a spectacular statement not of a prolegomenon to some future historical practice, but of one just undertaken. Like Gassendi's magnificent summary of Peiresc's research for the *History of Provence*, we know that each of Gassendi's sentences reflects the reality of Peiresc's archive. Moreover, joining as he did the language of love ("ardency") and scholarship ("curiosity") suggests that Gassendi, like Proust later, recognized the powerful life forces at work in even the most recondite historical research.

The history of Peiresc's "reception," as I have suggested elsewhere, is bound up with wider cultural changes.[43] Nevertheless, even a brief look at how the Crusades were studied in the immediate centuries after Peiresc can help us more clearly discern all his contribution. Du Chesne, as we have seen already, perceived the importance of the *Lignages d'Outremer*. When Antoine Galland published his friend Barthélemy d'Herbelot's *Bibliothèque Orientale* (1697) he suggested in the preface that study of sources, in particular Arabic sources, might shed additional light on the history of the Crusades.[44] In the middle of the eighteenth century, the Benedictines formulated a plan to publish Crusade monuments, not only texts but also documentation. And they, too, realized the need to have the Arab as well as the Western sources. The French Revolution intervened, and this project, along with many others, was dropped. Eventually the Academy of Inscriptions took it up and part of it fell, ultimately, to J.-F. Michaud, who brought Peiresc's comparative vision to some kind of fruition two centuries later—though a compendium of specifically *Arab* historians of the Crusades would not be published until 1969.[45]

But what we find neither in Michaud, nor in Friedrich Willken's nearly contemporary *Geschichte der Kreuzzüge* (7 vols., 1807–1832), nor in Heinrich von Sybel's cutting-edge *Geschichte des ersten Kreuzzugs* (1841), is a picture of the Crusades reconstructed from the ground up by way of archival documents. Michaud complained about not being able to find good narrative models in his literary sources and certainly not in the archives, even though he was not inclined to look there.[46] Von Sybel, like Droysen, heir to Ranke's revolution, may have begun with a section devoted to "Kritik der Quellen und der Literatur" but that it was entirely constituted by narratives suggests that up through this point archival, administrative documents were still not being used as sources for Crusade history.[47] What Peiresc had done would not be done again until the great historical revolution of the twentieth century. And even Braudel was given to wonder when "it will become possible to write general history from original documents and not from more or less secondary works."[48]

If, for the nearly sixty years since Momigliano's classic article of 1950, we have associated Renaissance antiquaries mucking about in ancient ruins with the beginnings of modern historiography, we need now to pay attention to them when they are wandering through churches or rifling through cartularies. In short, there is also a "Medieval History and the Antiquarian" to be written.[49]

Indeed, Momigliano himself flagged this story in his typical lapidary fashion, nodding in the direction of Mabillon "and his Italian disciples."[50] The importance increasingly attached to "historia sacra" for developing "modern" scientific history is fast filling in our knowledge of the antiquarian study of post-classical times.[51] There remains, nevertheless, a huge gap in our historiographical understanding, omitting the work of Peiresc, but also undervaluing the contributions of colleagues such as Andre Du Chesne and Henry Spelman, and followers like William Dugdale.[52] If we want to understand why, we might need to think in terms of literary, rather than forensic, expectations.

"Research" is a word that Peiresc, as we have seen, used repeatedly. If we think in terms of a semantic cloud, we see Peiresc associating the term with precision, detail, and curiosity. And he was a fantastic researcher. Yet just as we tend to take the practice of "research" for granted today—if even fifth-graders are assigned "research papers" can research really be that hard? or that complicated a notion?—we tend to overlook the prodigies of research performed in earlier times. Part of research, of course, is knowing what to look for; the other part is knowing where to look. Broadening the former, allows for greater success with the latter. Peiresc's work on the medieval Mediterranean demonstrates this time and again.

It makes sense, therefore, that there was nothing Peiresc appreciated more in a correspondent than when "he sets himself to narrate every little detail (*minutia*)."[53] Peiresc's acolyte, Gassendi, puts it more colorfully: "I'm not ashamed to communicate to you observations that are undercooked ("si peu cuisinées") because your spirit leads you to prefer the information straight up" ("des informations brutes").[54] Basic research, we might call this.

But there was also a literary consequence of this epistemological posture. Gassendi put into Peiresc's mouth praise of a travel account as "nuda storia."[55] He wanted facts, in as pure a format as possible. Peiresc's predilection for the unadorned, or unfiltered, fact was passed along to Gassendi, who described the beginning of his epochal biography of Epicurus as *nudam historiam*, a straightforward history, and its style as "nude recitata," or unadorned prose.[56] When Peiresc set about trying to explain to Cassiano dal Pozzo the kind of account of the 1631 eruption of Vesuvius that he wanted written, he stressed certain principles. What needed to be known was the precise time at which the principal events occurred, the "space of time" ("di spatio di tempo") in which they occurred, and "the time in which followed the most notable events" ("del tempo che successero gli accidenti più notabili"). With all this he thought it would be possible to establish "the correspondence of times and events and if there could be some dependence of the one on the other" ("corrispondenza de' tempi et de' momenti, se vi poteva essere alcuna dipendenza dell'uno all'altro").[57] The straightforward narration of events, in short, could establish causal relationships where none had been perceptible.[58]

Peiresc's *History of Provence* bears so little relationship to the brilliant research program that underpins it because when Peiresc chose to write a "History" he followed this understanding of the style most appropriate to its purpose. It left no space for his multilayered, multidirectional investigation. In the seesaw dialogue between research and writing, the seventeenth century saw the research side surge ahead. Olivier Poncet, for example, has described the research essays prepared by Jean Besly, Peiresc's correspondent, for his *Histoire des comtes de Poitou* as the better illustration of his excellence. Yet, Besly himself described these as coming together precisely "without a formed plan."[59] Nearly a century later, Leibniz, who spoke so compellingly about the ways in which history, and specifically medieval history, could be written from archival evidence, could do no better.[60] Although his research for the *History of the House of Brunswick*, like Peiresc's for *Provence*, glistens with brilliance, his written *History* is flat and dull.[61] Conventions of genre remained all-powerful; while the as yet uncanonized norms of research allowed for greater experimentation, they lacked a form of narrative exposition. It is only by putting the finished prose alongside the inevitably unfinished archive that we catch a glimpse of the historical whole that belies any comprehensive distinction between antiquaries and historians.

This gap between the writing of history and the researching of history, as de Certeau observed, first made itself evident in the era from Peiresc to Leibniz (we might want to extend it forward, beyond even Caylus, to Goethe). It poses a problem different from the one that Momigliano answered for us. He named Gibbon and Winckelmann as those who successfully, and finally, married the tools of the antiquary to the style of the rhetorically trained ancient historian. But de Certeau's periodization points to the development of that self-conscious sense of the difference between research and writing as a real and persistent dividing line. Thus, what passes for the history of scholarship c. 1800, the *historische Hilfswissenschaften* in German universities, acknowledged a distinction between historical work that belonged to the "describing sciences" (*Beschreibende Wissenschaften*), which comprised the post-antiquarian fields of geography, chorography, ethnography, Statistik, and the "narrating sciences" (*Erzählende Wissenschaften*), which included the history of culture, religion, and states.[62] De Certeau also urges us to reflect on the cost of creating that successful narrative. He sees the later history-writing as eliding the constructedness of historical knowledge; we might prefer to describe it in terms of a shift in emphasis away from a kind of curatorial intelligence that spins worlds from individual monuments toward an interpretative one that converts individual moments into longer narratives.

The literary dimension of research is uncharted terrain for historians of historiography but not, of course, for historians and theorists of fictional story-telling. The relationship between the describing and narrating modes— between research as the goal and narrative explanation as the goal—has been analyzed very carefully by Paul Ricoeur in *Time and Narrative*. He argues that there can be a "plot"—or expectation of a story—even in the research-driven projects, and he takes Braudel's *Mediterranean* as the most extreme example of this kind of unconventional narrative. "To be totally convincing, however," Ricoeur writes, "it is necessary to explain how history can still be a narrative when it stops being about events, whether it becomes structural, or comparative, or if it regroups into series items drawn from an atemporal continuum."[63] This is another way of asking our question about where Peiresc's kind of historical scholarship fits into the history of historiography, and when?

Ricoeur answers neither his question, nor ours. Like Rancière, his Braudel remains part of the grand tradition of narrative, though at its limit, where "what distinguishes the historian's concept of structure from that of the sociologist or the economist" is tested.[64] But Robert Alter, examining the history of the novel, did try to mark this line. Taking the long view, he argued that in the period highlighted by de Certeau, roughly from Cervantes to Sterne to Diderot, writers exposed the conventions and structure of their work, unwilling to hide them behind the scrim of narrative.[65] We would note that this resembles the way in which antiquaries wrote historical research in the same period—the great age of antiquarianism. It was in the nineteenth century, according to Alter, that the novel pretended to a mirror of reality and so buried its working parts. This aspect of Alter's argument rests, in turn, on the stunning essays of Eric Auerbach on Stendahl, Balzac, and Zola in *Mimesis*.[66] In the twentieth century, from Joyce onward, Alter writes, the mechanics and the overt experimentalism again came to the surface, denying any mimetic illusion. He concludes that the history of the novel, with its realistic telos, is therefore deeply, deeply flawed.

If we lay this alongside the conventional narrative of the history of history, whether Ludwig Wachler's in the early ninteenth century or Eduard Fuetter's in the early twentieth, we find a startling parallelism. Hayden White's *Metahistory* (1973), for all that it has come to appear as a disruptive work, is in fact deeply conservative. For it takes the whole history of history-writing for granted. Ranke, Michelet, Tocqueville, and Burckhardt, for him as for any turn-of-the-last-century German mandarin, are the best representatives of the practice of history. That White justifies this choice by representing them as expressing different dimensions of realism exactly corresponds to Alter's interpretation of the pretensions of the nineteenth-century novel.[67]

But if we follow Alter's lead, and take the longer view, these giants of history-writing now appear transformed (ironically) from canonical to exceptional. For in the preceding centuries we find the most exciting historical work being done by philologists and antiquaries, scholars who framed their research in terms of the analytical, the fragmentary, and the synchronic. And then again, in the twentieth century, from Warburg's *Mnemosyne Atlas* to Benjamin's *Passagenwerk* to the great collage that is Braudel's *Méditerranée* and beyond, we find these same framing devices casting new light on the dark parts of the cosmos of learning.

History, in the nineteenth century, and even more so the new discipline of archaeology, defined their practice against the antiquarian. "Archaeology," Champollion-Figeac wrote in 1833, "explains human monuments, and History finds there the princes and peoples about whom it speaks."[68] The recognition in the generations after Winckelmann that Prehistory was a field of inquiry that was only accessible through the study of things created a disciplinary self-image that has survived down to the present, aided by the diversion of the archaeology of the Greco-Roman and Egyptian and then Near Eastern worlds into the fields of Classics, Egyptology, and Assyriology. With this, the memory of any antiquarian ancestry was systematically expunged. Yet the more recent appeal of archaeology as cultural history, or in the archaeology of historical periods, or of archaeology oriented toward material culture, has created a research agenda resembling that of the pre-archaeological antiquarians.[69] Against this background, efforts to stress the descent of Archaeology from Antiquarianism, like those connecting antiquarianism to cultural history, do more than recover a forgotten parentage; they offer the possibility of turning an entire discipline upside down.[70]

Balzac's work, like Rodin's vision of the man, juts out like a headland on this turbulent coast. Presented as a realist by Auerbach and Alter, and as an "Archéologue" by a recent critic, his *Comédie Humaine* could seem the perfect example of the looming roadblock sitting between us and premodern approaches to the past.[71] Yet in fact it is by looking closely at "Balzac and Archaeology" that a path between past and present can be discerned in which the lure of realism seems part of the development of antiquarianism, rather than its nemesis.

Philippe Bruneau has surveyed the use, denotations, and connotations of "archaeology" and "antiquarianism" in Balzac, and demonstrated convincingly how Balzac's primary association of archaeology was with reconstruction—the old Paris in the age of the July Monarchy was slipping away as fast as old Roman marble in the kilns of Julius II—and identified "description" as its primary methodology. Balzac's "archaeology" referred to the range of human creations, up to and including the present, which were nevertheless out of step with the times, and therefore in danger of destruction. Objects of fashion necessarily stood outside the purview of archaeology, but so too, at the other extreme, did objects that were timeless, such as farm equipment. People could also be archaeological if they met the same criteria, as did, for example, Cousin Pons and the President Camusot.[72]

This kind of archaeology evokes Peiresc's interest in nonclassical fields (late antiquity, the middle ages), objects of no aesthetic intentionality (*si goffa maestria*), imagination (his *conjectures*), and constant engagement with Time the Destroyer (*Tempus Edax Rerum*). Peiresc's fascination with ritual and the relationship between objects and performance are also found in Balzac. "Archaeology," the latter wrote in 1834, "is to the social nature as comparative anatomy is to organized nature. A mosaic can reveal an entire society, just as the skeleton of an icthyosaurus all of creation. From one or another, all can be deduced, all is connected."[73] The real archaeologist, in short, did not excavate, nor seriate. The real archaeologist was the one who explained how the material and the living were related, and who did so by using his eye—but also his mind's eye.[74]

"Balzac and Archaeology," therefore, suggests a need to revise the history of archaeology to make for a less dramatic rupture—the *Société Française d'Archéologie* was founded in 1834, just as Balzac first formulated his grand plan for the *Comedie Humaine*. But "Balzac and Archaeology" also offers a way of rethinking the entailment between a certain kind of exposition (narrative) and a certain kind of history (narrative). Yet, the one nineteenth-century history that made explicit this connection between early modern antiquarianism and modern archaeology, Karl Bernhard Stark's *Handbuch der Archäologie der Kunst* (1880), is the one history of archaeology that is never cited by historians of archaeology.[75] And it took until the end of the twentieth century for another scholar, Michel Foucault, to revive Balzac's vision of archaeology as the study of the implied but invisible connections between visible but discontinuous relations.[76] As for the role of imagination in scholarly reconstruction, it remains today a touchy subject for historians, as recurring debates about historical fiction always remind us.[77]

If the nineteenth-century realist novel has come to define the genre, it has done so at a high price: both ignoring what came before, and also missing the link between the self-consciously experimental novels of the twentieth century that came after and those of the seventeenth and eighteenth that came before. So, too, as the form of history written from Gibbon to Burckhardt and, in some way on to Braudel, asserted itself as the standard it has occluded the achievements and ongoing influence of the early modern followers of Peiresc *and* obscured the genetic account that can link them to modernist historical experiments such as Benjamin's *Passagenwerk*. Similarly, archaeology's disavowal of its antiquarian paternity and insistence on prehistory as paradigm has made the continuity between early modern antiquaries and nineteenth-century novelists on the one hand, and moderns like Collingwood and Hodder on the other, almost completely invisible.[78]

If the nineteenth century, in short, far from defining the norm instead circumscribes the exception, then our deep inquiry into Peiresc's study of the medieval Mediterranean brings us to the brink of a momentous question: Could the antiquarian impulse—early modern *historia* with its inclination to research, reconstruction, and description—actually constitute a norm for the period 1500–2000 as a whole? This would be no less than a Copernican revolution in the history of historiography. It would suggest the need for a new morphology of antiquarianism that could account for its transformations over the arc of five centuries. This would need to be articulated in terms of practices but also presentation. And it would, in turn, make the nineteenth century into the "problem," the thing needing to be explained, rather than the standard against which early modern and modern deviations from a supposed norm are to be measured.[79]

Though once upon a time academic history may have successfully squeezed antiquarianism out of the university's precincts, the monograph of the twentieth century, in its evidentiary focus and narrow address, may have more in common with the research-mindedness of early moderns like Peiresc than with storytellers like Macaulay or Michelet. And all this leaves aside the uncontested dominance of the "antiquarian" in amateur and local history and the parahistorical genres of biography, memoire and historical fiction, as well as in successor disciplines such as archaeology and anthropology. Finally, Peiresc's refusal of story-telling for archiving, which may once have seemed like a radically distant form of writing, and his ranging across various media in his detective work, which once evoked the silent disdain of disciplinary border guards, now seem more familiar and much less radical in a scholarly age increasingly shaped by the curating and aggregating of information in searchable and linkable databases. The implications of this external transformation for future internalist histories of history can today only be guessed at.

Notes

[1] "Les armes de Hierusalem y estants meslees à cause que noz Comtes les avoient portees unies aux leurs durant trois cents ans, sans iamais les quitter." Carp., Bib. Inguimb., MS. 1864, fol. 307r.

[2] Peiresc makes the comparison in Carp., Bib. Inguimb., MS. 1811, fol. 26r.

[3] Benoit, "Les Porcellets de Syrie," 33.

[4] In the church of the Celestins in Paris, Peiresc identified Lusignan tombs (Carp. Bib. Inguimb., MS. 1793, fols. 26r–27r).

[5] In the Royal Library (shelfmark no. 714, Peiresc tells us) a life of St Louis contained several scenes that Peiresc labeled "COMMENT IL VA OULTRE MER," including one with detailed depiction of Saladin's Oriental costume (Carp. Bib. Inguimb., MS. 1779, fols. 15r-v). Peiresc's intense focus on the materiality of these illuminated manuscripts can be followed in *Documents parisiens sur l'iconographie de St. Louis*, Auguste Longnon, ed. (Paris: Champion, 1882).

[6] Peiresc discussed a cup that looked several hundred years old, with coats of arms of two Netherlandish families, the Aspremont and Cullembourg, engraved on its foot, which had been purchased by the Carthusians of Montrieu from the heirs of the late bishop of Marseille who had himself gotten it from people who had purchased it "in the Levant, whether at Rhodes or elsewhere." The white cross on a red field made the arms of Aspremeont, Peiresc commented, "but it could also relate to those of Rhodes or others of the Crusades." Carp., Bib. Inguimb., MS. 1771, fol. 265r.

[7] Notes on a conversation he had with Henri Poullain, avocat general en la Cour des Monnaies and author of *Traictes des Monnoyes* (Paris, 1621), conclude with an anecdote about a princess "ayant perdu son mary en Orient [*sic*], y portà à l'offrande des especes d'or Arabiques, dont elle fut blasmee" (Carp., Bib. Inguimb., MS. 1864, fol. 241r).

[8] Examples include a chivalric poem about Hugh de Tabarie (Carp., Bib. Inguimb., MS. 1793, fols. 649r–652v); Crusade chronicles, including Fulcher of Chartres, in the possession of Meric de Vic (Carp., Bib. Inguimb., MS. 1791, fols. 143–144). In the possession of Sr d'Arnaud of Forcalquier Peiresc found a manuscript of the French translation and continuation of William of Tyre's History of Jerusalem and had a copy made for himself (Carp., Bib. Inguimb., MS. 1792, fol. 250v). Peiresc noted that a continuator had taken up the story from the last chapter of book 22. Was he the first to notice this? For recent discussions of the continuation, and bibliography, see Peter W. Edbury, *The Conquest of Jerusalem and the Third Crusade: Sources in Translation* (Aldershot: Ashgate, 1996) and *Crusader Syria in the Thirteenth Century: The Rothelin Continuation of the History of William of Tyre with part of the* Eracles *or* Acre Text, (Aldershot: Ashgate, 1999). I thank Adam Kosto for bringing these references to my attention. This project can be dated to 1627. See Peiresc to Dupuy, 11 November 1627, *Lettres de Peiresc*, I, 407.

[9] For a comprehensive treatment of this theme, see the essays in *"Historia,"* Gianna Pomata and Nancy Siraisi, eds.

[10] "[D]etti commissioni, et deposto nell'archivio del Venaisiino dov'erano registrate le commissioni d'ambi le parte, così delle maestri Regii, come delli Apostolica,

Index

Index

❖

www.ingramcontent.com/pod-product-compliance
Lightning Source LLC
Chambersburg PA
CBHW080928100426
42812CB00007B/2409